Namesake Celebration

October 11, 2006

Namesake honorees; the names behind the faces:

Front Row (left to right)
Cannon, Helen
Faiss, Theresa
Faiss, Wilbur
Jeffers, Jay
Monaco, JoAnn
Heckethorn, Howard
Katz, Edyth
Von Tobel, Ed
Molasky, Irwin
Hickey Liliam
Thiriot, Joseph
Ober, D'Vorre
Ober, Hal
Givens, Linda Rankin
Hollingsworth, Howard
Goynes, Naomi
Parson, Stella

Second Row (left to right)
Escobedo Sr., Edmundo
Wolff, Elise L.
Steele, Judy
Hayes, Karen
Harney, Kathleen
Molasky, Susan
Lynch, Ann
Hill, Charlotte
Carl, Kay
Swainston, Theron
Twitchell, Neil
Watson, Rick
Iverson, Mervin
Fertitta, Victoria
Alamo, Tony
Goynes, Theron
Priest, Richard

Third Row (left to right)
Simmons, Eva
Harney, Tim
Greer, Edward A.
White, Thurman
Lamping, Frank
Jeffrey, Jack

Back Row (left to right)
Monaco, Mario
Lawrence, Clifford
Darnell, Marshall
Wallace, Matt
Tanaka, Wayne
Schorr, Steve
Mendoza, John F.
Mannion, Terry
Mannion, Jack
Gehring, Roger
Saville, Anthony
Bilbray, James
Dickens, Dusty
Roundy, Owen
Cortney, Francis
Ries, Aldeane
Johnston, Carroll
Bailey, Dr. William "Bob"

Education in the Neon Shadow

Education *in the* Neon Shadow

The First 50 Years of the Clark County School District

Stephens Press • Las Vegas, Nevada

Editor: Jami Carpenter
Contributing Authors: Kay Carl, John R. Gallifent, Jonathan Peters, Rick Watson
Research Assistant: Dana J. Benedict
Designer: Sue Campbell
Publishing Coordinator: Stacey Fott

Cataloging in Publication

Education in the neon shadow : the first 50 years of the Clark County School District / contributing authors, Kay Carl, John R. Gallifent, Jonathan Peters, Rick Watson : editor, Jami Carpenter.

   152 p. : photos ; 23 cm.

ISBN: 1-932173-83-8
ISBN-13: 978-1-932173-83-3

Beginning with the early settlements, and ending in 2005, this chronicles the history of the public schools in Clark County, Nevada.

1. Clark County School District (Nev.)—History. 2. Public schools—Nevada—Clark County—History. I. Carl, Kay. II. Gallifent, John R. III. Peters, Jonathan. IV. Watson, Rick. V. Carpenter, Jami, ed.

371.009'793'13   dc22   2009

STEPHENS PRESS, LLC
A Stephens Media Company

Post Office Box 1600
Las Vegas, NV 89125-1600
www.stephenspress.com

Printed in Hong Kong

To all who have dedicated their
careers and lives to public education
in Clark County.

Contents

Preface

The idea of creating a book about the Clark County School District's first fifty years was met with a great deal of enthusiasm, though it soon became apparent how difficult the task would be. There was no *one* place to gather the history; information was scattered throughout the county and much of it was in the memories of those who were the school district's pioneers.

Our efforts to bring the materials together for this book brought back many of our own recollections. We spent lots of time trying to remember someone's name, where a school building was or what it used to be called, and reminiscing about the many changes we have all seen in the district over the years. Through found documents, a photographic collection, and personal interviews, as well as patience and perseverance, we believe we have put together an interesting portrayal of the emergence of the Clark County School District.

Please note, however, that this book is not an encyclopedia of all of CCSD's accomplishments. A comprehensive analysis of the district's infrastructure is for another time, another book. Rather, our intent was to focus on specific challenges facing our schools, as well as showcase some of the unique features of our District.

We think we did our best to include accurate, historical, and interesting information; however, we may have unknowingly made errors and omissions, and for that, we apologize.

We hope this book will help you remember some of your experiences in the Clark County School District. We hope, too, that this book might serve as an introduction for the many new teachers and employees recruited to our rapidly growing district every year. We believe our work will help newcomers develop a sense of history and community, both of which are essential for those who will carry our traditions forward.

—Archive Committee

Introduction

One of the most prevalent and persistent themes in the Clark County School District's history is its growth. From the earliest days of the new school district to its present status as the nation's fifth largest, it has been a constant challenge to accommodate the flow of students coming into the county.

Student populations double decade after decade, and new schools continue to open, but it is difficult to keep pace. CCSD continually struggles, balancing the need for more buildings with limited budgets. The district has often resorted to creative solutions: In 1956, with over twenty thousand students, the newly-formed Clark County School District reverted to half-day, or double sessions. Ten years later, even with an aggressive building campaign, half of the almost sixty-three thousand Clark County students were still attending double sessions. And ten years after that, the battle for seats and funding remained. In fact, each decade since has faced the challenge of providing for steadily increasing student enrollment with slow-growing operational budgets.

Even with the passage of bonds, which provides funds for new construction and renovation of older school buildings, the operating budget must provide for staff, services, and supplies. So, while the taxpayers may support a new bond to build more schools, the state's educational budget often does not provide funds for more personnel, textbooks, or microscopes for the increased student population. Activities and special programs frequently bear the brunt of budget cuts, and unfortunately, many programs that are cut, such as middle school competitive sports, are never brought back.

The Clark County School District must also find, recruit, and hire hundreds of new faculty and staff every year. Unfortunately, the supply of qualified teachers often fails to match the demand of students. For the last several years, CCSD recruiters have traveled as far away as the Phillipines to entice teachers to move to the desert.

Just as teachers now come from around the world to the Clark County School District, students rep-

resent many different countries as well. There are 106 languages spoken in CCSD, representing 145 countries. By 2006, more than 48,000 were enrolled in English Language Learner (ELL) programs, with over eighty percent speaking Spanish.

Typically, residents flood into southern Nevada at the rate of five thousand a month, and the student population grows by twelve thousand to fifteen thousand enrollments every year. Only twice in its history has CCSD not met enrollment projections: The tragedy of September 11, 2001, which impacted the Las Vegas tourism industry, affecting job opportunities; and the sub prime mortgage practices that began in 2007, putting the housing market in Clark County in crisis. Yet even though growth slowed, the student population still increased.

New resorts and industries are slated to open in the coming years, bringing another influx of families into the Las Vegas valley, Mesquite, and Coyote Springs. As history has shown, the Clark County School District will continue to struggle to meet the educational needs of these new residents until someday, hopefully, Nevada students become the state's number one priority.

Education in the Neon Shadow is the story of the Clark County School District's efforts to harness the energy of southern Nevada's growth. It is the story of a desert community and the influence of local, national, and world events in shaping the programs that distinguish this district.

The old Mormon Fort as it appears today.

CHAPTER 1

Early History

In 1826, Jedediah Smith, fur trapper and adventurer, passed through the area now known as southern Nevada. In 1829, Mexican traders traversed the twelve hundred miles of high mountains, arid deserts, and deep canyons with their pack mules from the old outpost at Santa Fe, New Mexico through the Las Vegas valley to El Pueblo de Los Angeles in California on what later became the Spanish Trail. John C. Fremont, US Army officer, surveyor, and map maker spent several days in the valley during his exploration of the West in 1844. After returning home, he published and distributed twenty thousand copies of a map showing Las Vegas as an important stop on the way West.

As part of Utah territory, Nevada history begins in 1851, when less than a hundred settlers gathered at Mormon Station (now Genoa) to organize a squatter government. By 1854, the governor and Legislative Assembly of the territory of Utah set the boundaries for the new Nevada territory with the southern boundary being set at the 37th degree of latitude.

In 1855, thirty Mormon missionaries from the Church of Jesus Christ of Latter day Saints in Salt Lake City, Utah, were sent to Las Vegas to establish a friendly relationship with the Indians of the area, to teach them the gospel and how to farm. They also built a fort that provided a way station between southern California and the Salt Lake valley.

After the mission had been established a short time, the families arrived and educating the children began. The first classes were held on September 21, 1856, in a space used as a meeting room and storehouse in the fort. The first teacher was Alexander A. Lemon, who instructed the Indian students along with the missionaries' children. A tax of three dollars a quarter was assessed for each of the missionaries' children, but by the end of 1856 most of the missionaries had returned to Salt Lake City. The remaining missionaries were called home to Utah in 1857 and the fort was abandoned. The Old Fort land fell into the hands of other owners who went on to develop a ranch and farm.

In 1859, a constitutional convention was held in Genoa where a declaration of rights and a constitution

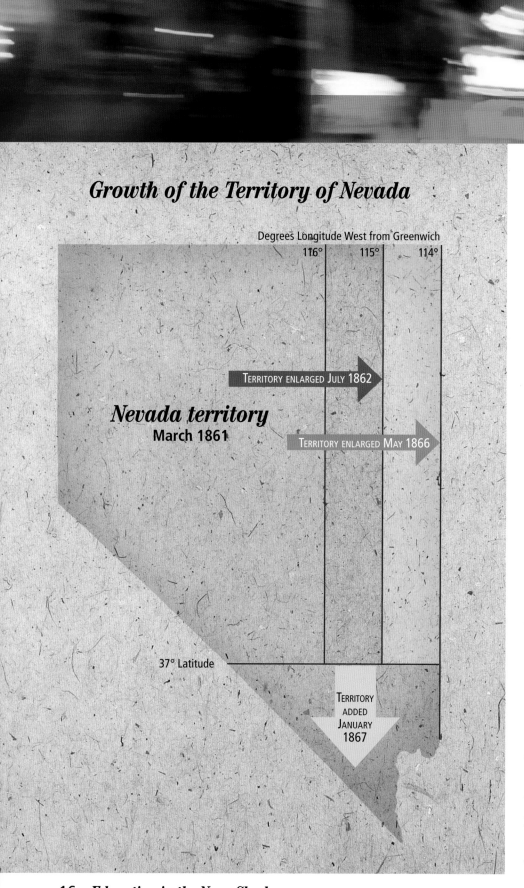

Growth of the Territory of Nevada

Degrees Longitude West from Greenwich

116° 115° 114°

Nevada territory
March 1861

TERRITORY ENLARGED JULY 1862

TERRITORY ENLARGED MAY 1866

37° Latitude

TERRITORY ADDED JANUARY 1867

were adopted, which were presented to the people of the new territory in September 1859 and accepted. The territory of Nevada was organized by an act of Congress in 1861 and in 1862, Nevada territory was enlarged by one degree east into Utah territory.

Nevada was granted statehood in 1864. In May 1866, Congress granted one more degree east to 114 degrees longitude to include the land which Nevada had laid claim. It also expanded the boundary as far south as the Colorado River, which included all of the Arizona territory lying between the river and the southern line of Nevada. In January 1867, the Nevada legislature formally accepted the gift of the area south of the original boundary. This portion of land became part of the existing Lincoln County, and in 1909, Clark County was established from the southern portion of Lincoln County.

Agrarian Settlements

St. Thomas

Unlike the Las Vegas valley, the Muddy River valley, sixty miles north of Las Vegas, had plenty of water and fertile soil. Mormon families from southern Utah moved into the valley to establish St. Thomas on January 8, 1865. The site was located near the confluence of the Muddy and Virgin Rivers on their way to the Colorado River.

The settlers built a school shortly after settling the area. The adobe building was roughly twelve by fourteen feet, and could hold twenty-five to thirty students. It remained in existence until 1915 and was replaced by a two-story brick building with

St. Thomas School, circa 1915–1933.

Logandale School, circa 1935–1956.

four classrooms and an auditorium on the second floor, which was used until the end of the 1932–33 school year. The school and most other buildings in St. Thomas were dismantled for use elsewhere. The rising waters of Lake Mead created by the building of Hoover Dam in 1935 eventually flooded the remainder of the community.

Logandale

Between 1865 and 1870, Mormon families also moved into the Muddy Valley region now known as Logandale, Overton, and Moapa. They also created other small communities that no longer exist such as Mill Point, Kaolin, and Simonville. While schools were certainly part of these early settlements, there are few historical records due to loss through fire, floods, and time. We do know that education was important to these Mormon settlers and that quite often, long before there was a dedicated school building, classes were held in the homes of the settlers and taught by the women in the community. As the number of students in the community grew and funds were raised, a school building was built and a regular teacher was hired.

In Logan, as the settlement was known until 1917, the first school building was erected about 1899. In 1919, all small school districts in the Moapa and Virgin Valley area were consolidated into Educational District No. 1. The new district orchestrated the construction of a Moapa Valley elementary and high school in Overton. All Logandale students attended the new school in Overton from 1920 to 1935. A new school was built in Logandale in 1935, made from native stone quarried in the area. The school had four classrooms and a gymnasium. By 1938, an addition was needed to make room for the seventh and eighth graders, which was added to the front of the building using the bricks salvaged from the St. Thomas school. The school became the activity center for the community and served until it closed in 1956, when once again the Logandale children were bused to Overton.

Under the newly consolidated Clark County School District, the building was opened every spring in the 1960s and 70s to provide educational opportunities for the transient farm workers' children. The building was later renovated and used as a community center and recreation hall for the town of Logandale.

Unable to care for the property and building, the center returned to the CCSD in 1988. It remained boarded up until 1997 when an agreement between the CCSD and the Old Logandale Historical and Cultural Society took up the renovation that brought it to the restored condition we see today. It houses a wide selection of artifacts, documents, and photographs that depict the history of the Moapa Valley.

The new Grant Bowler Elementary School was built in Logandale in 1980.

St. Joseph

St. Joseph had a school in 1865. In August 1868, two young boys built a fire in back of one of the homes to roast potatoes. A breeze caught the fire and blew sparks to the tule-thatched roof of one building, which started a fire that consumed most of the fort, including the school. After that, there is no record of a school in St. Joseph until 1892 when the second floor of a granary was used for the school, church, and community activities.

About 1899, a new school building was constructed, referred to as the boxcar school, as it was twelve feet wide and twenty-four feet long and was used until 1910. Soon after, a new building was erected in Logan and was used until 1920 when a school was built in Overton.

Overton

Martha Cox was the first known teacher in the Muddy Valley area. She arrived in 1881 after taking the teachers' examination in Pioche, the government center for Lincoln County.

When she arrived in Overton, the adobe school was not ready for students. Instead of postponing instruction, Ms. Cox held classes outside. Across from the school site, three large trees shaded a flattened terrain along the stream. She hung a blackboard from one of the trees and began giving instruction to nine students.

Just as there was no school, Ms. Cox had no place to live, either. She used an empty cotton storage shed as her house. She had to do all of her cooking over a fire outside. She also milked her neighbors' cows in return for some milk for herself. When she wasn't teaching, she picked cotton and helped with other crops in the valley.

Without a proper building, classes moved from home to home before the two-room adobe building with a thatched roof was finished. A tent was set up next to it to accommodate all the students. When the area flooded in 1889–90 and the school was surrounded by water, a one-room long adobe building was built outside the flood area.

Later, in 1902, the community built a brick building that served its educational needs for ten years. When a larger facility was needed, they built a two-story block structure in 1914 that could house all twelve grades. In 1922, additions were made that included a 250-seat auditorium on the first floor and a gymnasium on the floor above. Over time, more additions and improvements were made until it was finally torn down in 1950 to make way for a more modern build-

ing that was finished in 1951. After decades of use this building was remodeled and is now the W. Mack Lyon Middle School, and at a new site, the Moapa Valley High School was built in Overton in 1993.

Moapa

The Moapa settlement on the upper Muddy Valley River first held school classes in 1893 with Dreene Gaud as teacher for the 1893–94 school term. When the railroad was completed through Moapa in 1905, a one-room school opened. It had two small store rooms in front, one for books and supplies and the other for coal. This building was used until 1926 when a new school was built on the west side of town; it could accommodate more students from the area, including the children of railroad workers and ranch families, as well as children from the Moapa River Indian reservation, who had previously been schooled under the supervision of an Indian agent on the reservation. During a later remodeling, the structure was weakened and was abandoned in 1951. From this period on, the educational needs of the area were provided by busing students to Overton.

Other small schools existed in the area; in 1915, enough people had settled in the Warm Springs area that a one-room school was built on the home ranch about seven miles from Moapa and operated from 1905 until 1922. Another, first known as Crystal and renamed Dry Lake School in 1945, operated from 1926 to 1953.

Today this community has grown with the addition of some manufacturing activity and a power plant in the area and is served by the Ute Perkins Elementary School built in 1990.

Bunkerville

A company of pioneers from Santa Clara, Utah, led by Edward Bunker and his family, established a Mormon

Overton School, circa 1905.

Dry Lake School, circa 1926.

drove four posts into the ground. They then lashed the poles at head height and covered this "roof" with green willow branches. The structure wasn't used often, though; students were often too busy helping on family farms, and the weather was often too cold to hold classes in the brush structure.

Things improved when the community built an adobe structure with windows and wood floors to serve as a combination church, dining hall, and school. The roof, however, was still thatched, and couldn't stand up against foul weather. In class, children sat on benches made of split cottonwood logs pulled up to a long table. The teacher, Samuel O. Crosby, owned one spelling book, one arithmetic book, and two readers. From these meager tools, he taught his students.

In 1880, Bunkerville had 125 residents with thirty-three pupils attending the school. Recognizing the need for an extended educational program, Myron Abbott taught night school to the boys and men who spent days working in the fields.

In 1890, Martha Cox moved from Overton to teach in the Bunkerville School. In 1894, she had so many students that she applied for a teacher's assistant.

colony, appropriately named Bunkerville, along the Virgin River on January 6, 1877.

In less than two years, enough people had joined the new colony to warrant a school. The community dining hall served as the first school on November 5, 1878. Four months later, the first school term ended.

The townsfolk decided to build a dedicated school building to free-up space in their meeting and dining hall, but they didn't have the resources or time to construct a permanent structure. Instead, they

Early student transportation.

Mrs. J. I. Earl agreed to serve in this role for five dollars a month.

The growth continued, so in 1900, a third teacher was hired to conduct classes in private homes while a new church/schoolhouse was built. This new building was seventy-five by one-hundred feet and was built with rocks carried from the surrounding hills. When the structure was completed, one of the townspeople, Joseph I. Earl, bragged that the new building was the best schoolhouse in Lincoln County (Clark County was not established until a few years later). James S. Abbott said Bunkerville had outdone the entire United States when it came to tax levies for schools. He claimed the school building was the best in the whole country.

This new facility served the community until it caught fire in 1921. The inside was totally gutted, leaving only the rock walls.

The townspeople rallied after this tragedy. They built a second rock school. When the school walls were completed, Joseph I. Earl traveled to Carson City to receive three-hundred dollars from Senator Francis Newlands for the purpose of placing a roof over the structure.

It wasn't until 1911 that the first high school in the Bunkerville area was established. Fifteen secondary students studied domestic science, physical science, and social science. Prior to the creation of the high school, students had to attend Las Vegas High School, the only high school in southern Nevada. While they attended, the girls lived in a dormitory on Fremont Street while the boys lived in private homes through-

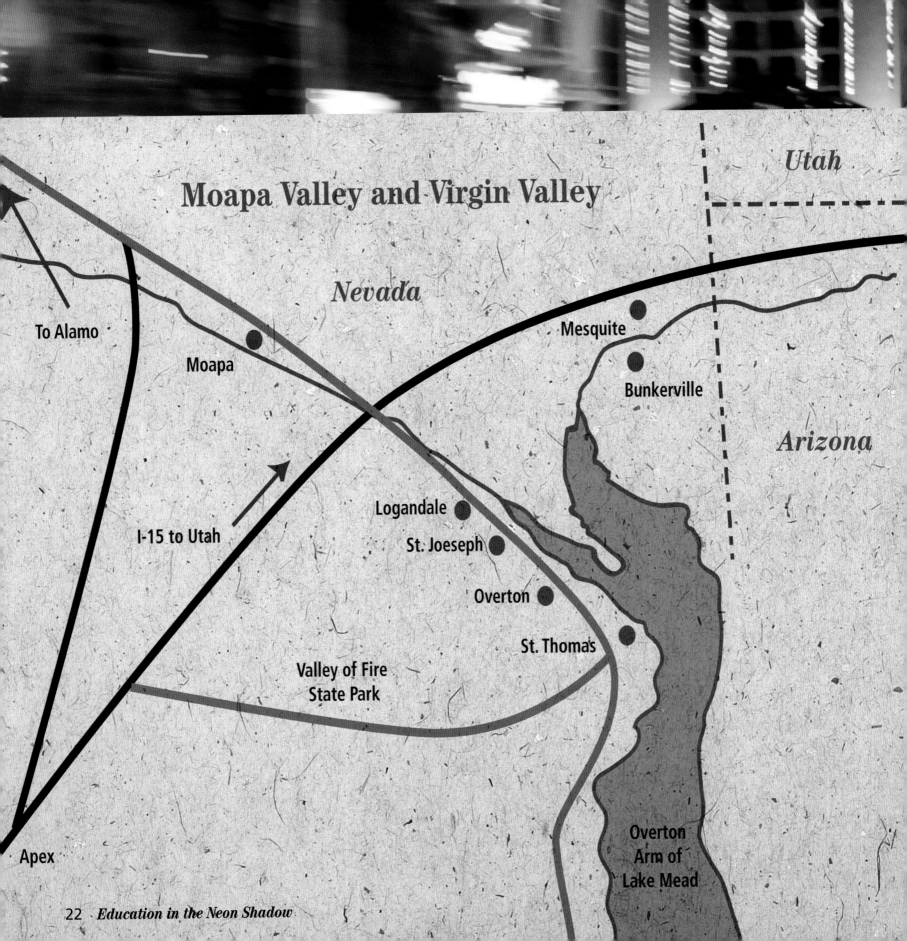

Moapa Valley and Virgin Valley

Utah

Nevada

To Alamo

Moapa

Mesquite

Bunkerville

Arizona

I-15 to Utah

Logandale

St. Joeseph

Overton

St. Thomas

Valley of Fire
State Park

Apex

Overton
Arm of
Lake Mead

out the small town of Las Vegas, using the seven and a-half-dollars allowance they received each month from the county to pay for their room and board.

In 1917, Bunkerville began construction on a wood frame building to house the new high school, but a strong wind nearly demolished the structure. Instead of repairing the damage, the townspeople raised enough money to build a concrete school on the same spot. In the meantime, the original elementary schoolhouse burned down. Classes were moved into the church, which also burned down on December 6, 1920. No books, equipment, or records survived the fire.

The residents of Bunkerville focused their efforts on completing the new concrete schoolhouse. When it opened for classes, the school boasted a gas lighting system, a recreational hall, an office, and a library. Shortly thereafter, a gymnasium and four more classrooms were added.

Finally, Bunkerville had a school building that would survive fire and storms. The new school has served their educational needs for decades without any of the tragedies that plagued earlier school structures.

Mesquite

In 1880, Mormon settlers moved onto the Mesquite Flat that runs along the Virgin River. By 1882, fifteen families were living in Mesquite. There were enough school-aged children among those families to warrant a teacher.

Lucius Peck, the postmaster and store helper for Mesquite, volunteered to hold classes in his home. This arrangement worked well until floods and stifling hot weather caused the initial settlers to abandon their small community along the river in 1893.

People didn't stay away from Mesquite for long. By 1895, people were moving back to the area. This time, Lorena Hardy was the teacher and classes were held in her home until Jessie Waite offered his larger home as a temporary school.

When classes began in 1897, a large tent served as the town's school. Finally, in 1909, a church was built that served as a more permanent home for the school. And later, in 1923, a concrete structure acted as both a community meetinghouse and school.

The community continued to grow and became a large farming community in the northeast corner of Nevada, near the Nevada-Utah border. Eventually, it was established enough to erect a building for the single purpose of education. Today, through expanded gaming and recreation facilities, the community has grown large enough to have a high school, a middle school, and an elementary school.

Early Mining Settlements

The allure of gold, silver, and other minerals attracted many men to Nevada seeking their fortune. Mines were scattered throughout the state, including the southern tip. A few mines developed some permanency and towns formed nearby. Unlike agricultural communities, mining towns were slow to attract families and often struggled to accommodate the educational needs of the children who ended up in the mining camps. Eventually, the more stable mining towns established schools, even school districts, though these educational efforts

Top: Searchlight, 1910. Note school on knoll. Bottom right: A poem offering "advice" to new teachers in the early years.

often struggled to stay open from term to term.

Today, while most of these towns and schools have disappeared, a few remain. Though not as large as schools in nearby cities, these smaller schools often have a tenacious spirit of survival.

Searchlight

Shortly after G.F. Colton discovered gold on May 6, 1897, the town of Searchlight was born. By October 1898, a camp was formed and a post office was established. The following year, the community opened a school for its few children. These students met in a small shared structure until the new twenty by forty foot wood frame building was constructed in 1904.

By 1906, however, the school was in need of more space and construction began on a two-room addition to the

THE WAY IT WAS
RULES FOR NEVADA TEACHERS

Thou shalt live in single blessedness or thy contract will be void.

Thou shalt attend community dances and trip the light fantastic with local swains.

Thou shalt do janitorial service and keep the schoolhouse neat and clean.

Thou shalt build a fire so that the schoolhouse is warm upon the arrival of students.

Thou shalt put on programs for community entertainment at Christmas and other holidays.

Thou shalt always maintain a good example of conduct and dress for thy pupils.

Thou shalt register non-partisan and avoid political involvement.

Thou shalt stay off the streets after 9 P.M. on weekdays unless for a worthy cause.

Thou shalt remain in town on weekends unless given permission to leave by the schoolboard.

Thou shalt attend social gatherings lest thou appear to be snobbish.

Searchlight school, 1938.

structure. By 1908, the school had 101 students. But with the decline in mining a few years later, Searchlight became a near ghost town. By 1927, there were only five students among the fifty residents.

In the boom-bust nature of mining, the town experienced a rebound in the late 1930s. With optimism about where the town was headed, the residents built a new cement-block school on the same site in 1942. But the optimism was short-lived. By end of the decade, student enrollment had dropped back down again.

The schoolhouse remained in use until 1992 when the Harry Reid Elementary School was built nearby to replace the original, which was falling apart, couldn't handle new technology, and didn't have space for elementary special programs, such as music and art. This new school was named for one of the most well-known Nevada students to attend the Searchlight school, US Senate Majority Leader Harry Reid.

Nelson

Native Americans knew about the gold and silver stores in Eldorado Canyon centuries before Europeans entered the region. Spanish explorers began mining the area as early as the 1700s. American miners arrived as late as 1857. By 1862, a full-fledged gold rush descended upon Eldorado Canyon.

Nelson School, circa 1930s.

This building served as the teacher's residence for Nelson School.

There were many criminals and Civil War deserters among the residents of the early mining camp. As a result, there was a general lack of a justice system in the area. This environment was made worse as feuds broke out with Indians living around the camp. In 1867, the little community asked the US Army for help to protect the camp.

While World War II ended industrial mining in the area, independent miners continued to work the area through the 1960s. Over the course of time, mining activity in the area produced more than four million dollars in gold and silver, which were extracted from the ground in and around Eldorado Canyon.

Many of the families of the miners in Eldorado Canyon lived in Nelson. While there is no record of when the Nelson schoolhouse was built, classes were held there as early as 1926. In the 1927 school year, six students attended classes. By 1937, enrollment quadrupled to twenty-four students. At its height, in 1942, the Nelson school had thirty-seven students. By 1944, however, that number dropped to only thirteen students. From that point on, the school never had more than twenty students and in the early 50s, classes ceased there altogether. In 1967, the property was sold and the school building was dismantled by the new owners. Today Nelson is a small community of thirty to forty people, mostly retired, who enjoy the quiet canyon life only fifty miles south of Las Vegas.

Sandy Valley

West of Goodsprings, several mines were developed. Gold, silver, copper, lead, and zinc were extracted from the mountain foothills around Sandy Valley. While there have been residents in the area since 1893, their numbers have significantly declined since mining activity dwindled during the 1930s.

A school operated in Sandy Valley off and on from 1911 through 1935. The Bartine School District was organized in 1936 to sup-

Students at Sandy Valley, 1927.

Sandy Valley, 1938.

Sandy Valley students raise the flag, 1982.

port this fledgling school. The following year its name changed to the Spring Mountain School District.

As mining activities wound down and people moved away, students throughout the defunct school district were sent to Goodsprings. The community of Sandy Valley sprang back, however, as aviation enthusiasts moved to homes surrounding the community's airstrip, and casino expansion at Primm brought other desert dwellers into the valley. In 1982, the Clark County School District opened the Sandy Valley Elementary and Middle School, and in 2007, it opened a high school in the town that was once so small it couldn't support a school.

Goodsprings

In 1886, lead and zinc mines emerged around the area southwest of Las Vegas. By 1892, as many as two hundred miners were camped in the area that would become known as Goodsprings.

Left: Goodsprings School in 1915.

Right: Goodsprings School bell in 1981.

Left: Blue Diamond School, circa 1930.
Right: Blue Diamond teacher and students.

A town was established in 1899 when a post office was built and community life emerged. The townspeople formed their first school in 1907. Initially, classes were held in a tent while the students and teacher, Winifred Hardy, waited for a schoolhouse to be built. Classes continued to be taught in different locations until a permanent building was erected in 1913. The bell on the roof called children to the one-room school that included a library. Plumbing consisted of a hand water pump in the front of the building and two outhouses in back. Electric lines were installed in 1914. The first teacher in the new building, Katherine Williams, was paid one hundred dollars a month including five dollars for her janitorial duties.

The school cost the town two thousand dollars to build. By 1916, the town had grown so much that two rooms had to be added to the structure. The original room was then used for school programs, club socials, and other community events. Today, the Goodsprings School is on the the National Register of Historical Places as the oldest Clark County school that was built as a school and still holds classes.

Even as urban sprawl pushes closer to this community, it still maintains the aura of a small, frontier town.

Blue Diamond

One of the oldest, continually running elementary schools in Clark County is the Blue Diamond Elementary School. It is located on land that was originally known as the Cottonwood Ranch which encircled Cottonwood Springs.

Early in the twentieth century, prospectors dis-

School Districts in 1955

All of the smaller local school districts listed below were consolidated into the Clark County School District in 1956.

Blue Diamond
Boulder City Union
Boulder City High School
Educational Consolidated District 1
Moapa Valley High School
Virgin Valley High School
Eldorado (Nelson)
Enterprise (Arden)
Garnet
Goodsprings
Basic High School
Indian Springs
Las Vegas Union
Las Vegas High School
Paradise
Searchlight
Sloan
Whitney

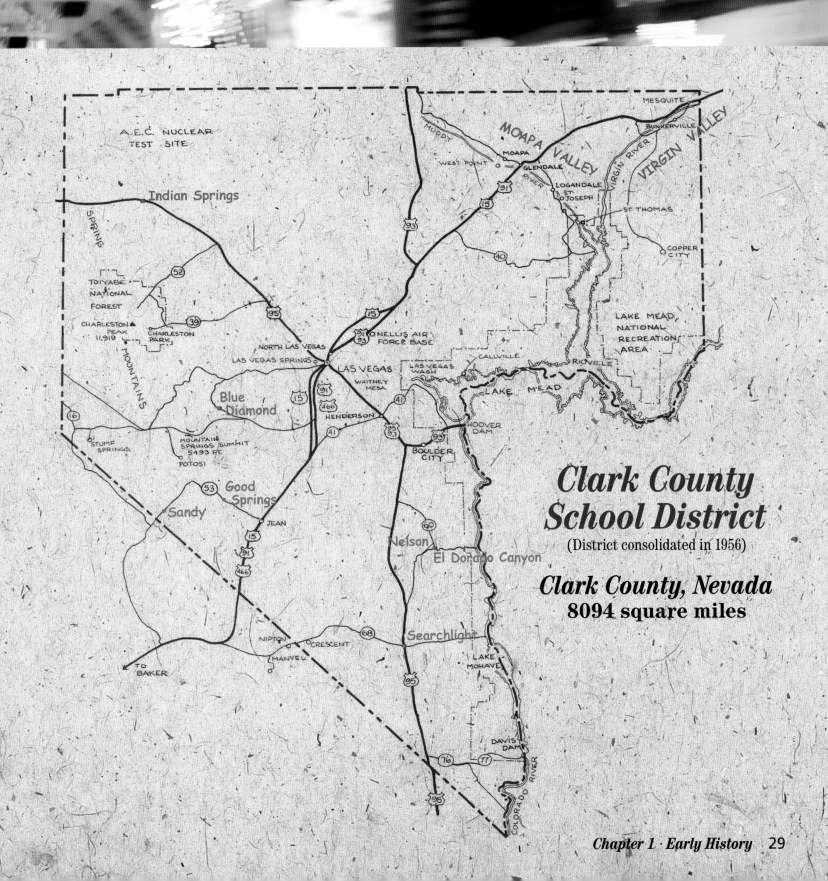

**Clark County
School District**

(District consolidated in 1956)

Clark County, Nevada
8094 square miles

covered high-quality gypsum in the hills around Cottonwood Ranch. Later, the Blue Diamond Company purchased the mining rights for the gypsum mines as well as the ranch as the ideal place to build a town for the mine workers and their families.

In 1929, the community built a small elementary school on the ranch. Later, classes were held up the hill, near the mine, but returned to the village in 1942 when the Blue Diamond School District was formed.

Today Blue Diamond is a small community located at the southern end of the Red Rock National Recreation Area.

Indian Springs

Forty miles northwest of Las Vegas sits Indian Springs, a small community of about thirteen hundred residents. The town was named for the artesian spring that provides water to the area and had been used by Native Americans. The Las Vegas and Tonopah railroad had facilities there from 1906 to 1919, after which that service was discontinued.

Indian Springs schoolhouse 1923–1931. Below: Indian Springs, circa 1918.

By 1927, a school existed on and off through the next two decades. In 1941, the Army Air Force opened a training area at Indian Springs, which closed in 1947 and reopened in 1948 as an auxiliary air field to Nellis Air Force Base. In 1956, the educational facilities of the small community became part of the Clark County School District and by 1968 a new school was constructed that eventually housed all grades through high school. Today Indian Springs is the home of the renamed Creech Air Force Base, which is used by the USAF Thunderbirds and

Las Vegas Schools — 1935

Schools located to the north.
(Not shown on the map.)

Westside School (1921), branch of Las Vegas Grammar School. Washington and D St.

Washington School (1921) N. Las Vegas, No.1.

Jefferson School (1942) N. Las Vegas No. 2 (part of the Washington School)

First Las Vegas School (1905) 2nd & Lewis.

Kindergarten (1921) Bridger & 4th St.

North

South

Bridger Avenue

Clark Avenue

Fifth Street

Fifth Street

Aerial photo taken in 1935.

Block 37—Buildings backed by Fifth Street.

Kindergarten 1921

Las Vegas Grammar School–1910
Housed first through twelfth grades until 1917.

The first high school classes were held in this building.

Manual Arts 1921

Tent School 1934–1936

Las Vegas Grammar School–1936
(Known as Fifth Street School.)
Front faces East to Fifth Street.

Las Vegas High School 1917
Housed 6th, 7th, & 8th grades after 1930. Destroyed by fire in 1934.

Buildings faced Fourth Street.

Block 37 was designated for public use when the Las Vegas Land & Water Company auctioned lots in 1905.

Las Vegas Grammar School (1910–1917) 1st through 12th grades until 1917.

Manual Arts HS (1921)

Tents used for temp classrooms after fire.

Shell of Las Vegas HS Built in 1917, burned in 1934 while being used for 7th and 8th grades.

Site of Fifth St. School (built 1936)

Las Vegas High School (1930)

Future site of Las Vegas HS Auditorium (built 1954)

is home to the USAF Predator, an unmanned aerial vehicle.

Industrial Towns

A person surveying Clark County today might miss the influence that industry had in building the county and attracting people from across the nation to the remote desert.

Las Vegas exists because of a rail line that ran from Salt Lake to Los Angeles. The early steam engines needed water to operate, and the Las Vegas Springs was the only significant city water source for many miles in any direction.

Boulder City exists because of the Hoover Dam and the importance of downstream flood control and the generation of electric power that contributed to the economic and industrial growth of the southwest. Henderson would not exist today if it were not for the industrial metal needs of the country during World War II.

The current landscape of tourism benefitted from the initial support of industry that established a population and the resources to support a new economy.

North Las Vegas

Originally named Vega Verde, North Las Vegas was founded in 1918 when Tom Williams, Sr., moved his family from Utah and bought 150 acres of land bordering the north boundary of the Helen J. Stewart Ranch. By 1932, enough families with children had settled into the area that the Las Vegas Union School District approved construction of a primary school at the corner of White Street and College Avenue

(Lake Mead Boulevard) on land donated by Tom Williams. In 1942 two temporary rooms were added and by 1948 a four-room block addition was built on the property. Named the North Las Vegas School No. 1, it was changed to Washington School in 1949.

In 1946, North Las Vegas was incorporated and by 1950 there were almost 3900 residents. By 1960, there were over 18,000 and in 2007 there were 215,000 residents. As the community grew additional schools were built: J.D. Smith, which opened in 1952 as an elementary school; Rancho High School in 1954; Lincoln Elementary School in 1955; and Tom Williams Elementary School in 1957. Today more than thirty-five schools serve the eighty-two square mile area of North Las Vegas that stretches across the northern rim of the Las Vegas Valley, the fourth largest city in Nevada.

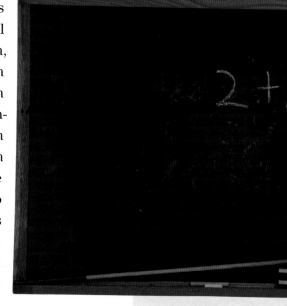

Las Vegas

At the beginning of the twentieth century there was no railroad linking Salt Lake City with Los Angeles, but the growing population in these two cities made commercial transportation between the two highly desirable. The distance required several train stops in between for water and maintenance. William Clark, a US Senator from Montana, purchased the San Pedro, Los Angeles, and Salt Lake railroads with the goal of laying track all the way to Salt Lake

Las Vegas' first school building, circa 1905. Inset: the building was destroyed by fire in 1910.

The Methodist Church substituted as the school after the 1910 fire.
Below: Las Vegas Grammar School, 1910.

Student body of Las Vegas Grammar School, which housed grades 1–12, circa 1912.

City. He also bought the 1800 acre Stewart Ranch from Helen J. Stewart, which included the springs, the ranch's water source. His vision was to have a stop in Las Vegas with a major train yard, switching station, repair shops, ice house, and a town for the railroad employees.

He had a competitor, however; Edward Harriman of the Union Pacific Railroad was determined to do the same, but was coming from Utah. An agreement was reached between Clark and Harriman and train service from Los Angeles to Salt Lake City was completed in May 1905.

On May 15, 1905, the railroad company held an auction to sell lots in the new town. People arrived from all over, pursuing promises of cheap land in a new boomtown. As the sun rose on that day, so did the temperature. When temperatures reached 110 degrees at three p.m., the auction was postponed until the following morning.

Before the auction could continue the next day, construction was already underway in the new town. Unfortunately, the funds that were originally set aside to build a school were diverted to build a much needed jail, so classes were held that first year in a tent along the Las Vegas Creek. The tent was large enough to admit seventeen students. The trees originally planted by the Mormon missionaries in 1855 provided shade for the young scholars.

Plans for a new school on the corner of Second and Lewis were scrapped when the Salt Lake Hotel came up for sale. The townspeople realized that the old hotel could be purchased for $150 and moved to the school site for less than the cost of building a new school from the ground up. The thirty by forty-

Las Vegas Grammar School students, circa 1911.

eight foot hotel was converted into two classrooms for a total cost of $550. The students themselves raised the money for a bell and belfry to complete the school building.

Classes started on October 2, 1905, but the classrooms were crowded by mid-October with eighty-one students. In what would become a trend for Las Vegas, the school was bursting with 114 students by the end of November. The original tent school had to be moved next to the new school to act as an overflow classroom. When the school ran out of money early in the school year, classes ended at the end of March and the school officially closed on April 26, 1906.

The short school year motivated the townspeople to support their educational system. Not only was enough money raised to fund a full school year the next fall, but there was also enough money to build an addition for a library.

Even with the addition, the school trustees realized there wouldn't be enough room to handle the new students coming to Las Vegas. Therefore, plans were made for a third building, one that would solve the overcrowding problem once and for all.

Clark County High School Girls Basketball team, 1912. Imagine playing in these outfits.

Clark County High School building, circa 1918.

The first students completed eighth grade in Las Vegas in 1907. There was not a convenient option for attending high school. The students in the communities along the Muddy and Virgin Rivers traveled to Utah for high school, but for Las Vegas students, the distance to Utah was too great.

In 1909, two years later, the Board of Education agreed to hold high school classes in the nearby Methodist Church. Parents were charged five dollars for these high school classes.

To support the fledgling town, the Las Vegas Land and Water Company, a division of the Union Pacific Railroad, donated property for a new school on the corner of Fourth and Bridger Streets. Block 37, which had been reserved for public use when the town's parcels were originally laid out, was deeded to the Las Vegas School District for a ten dollar gold coin. The block extended from Bridger Street to Lewis Street between Fourth and Fifth Streets. The new grammar school was built on the north half of the block. Even though it faced Fourth Street, it became known as the Fifth Street School.

Unfortunately, months before the new school was ready, the old hotel/school burned down in December 1910. While it could not be proven, people believed the fire was set intentionally. Classes quickly moved back to the Methodist Church and a boarding house next door for the rest of the school year. It was the first of many times that a Las Vegas school accommodated overcrowding with half-day sessions. To maximize classroom space, half the students attended classes in the mornings while the other half attended in the afternoons.

The new Las Vegas Grammar School dominated the architecture of Las Vegas. In a town that resembled many rural outposts of the time, the mission-style architecture of the two-story school stood in contrast to the surrounding buildings. The school was a concrete structure with a metal roof to prevent future fires. On a date that has significance today, the building opened for classes on September 11, 1911.

Many people believed the school was too large and that there would never be enough children in Las Vegas to fill it. After all, the school had fourteen class-

Las Vegas High School circa, 1931.

Westside neighborhood between C and D Streets at Monroe Avenue.

Fire destroyed the old Las Vegas High School on May 14, 1934.

Fifth Street School, built in 1936.

When Las Vegas was first formed, a separate town already existed on the west side of the tracks. J.T. McWilliams was a surveyor who arrived in 1904 and promptly laid out what he called the McWilliams Townsite. The area became known as the westside of the tracks and then simply the Westside. Black employees of the railroad company were among the first to live in Westside, though their children attended classes on the east side of the tracks, as there was no school on the Westside until 1922.

From early on, music played an important part in Clark County schools.

Las Vegas Grammar School, circa 1940 .

The oldest remaining school in the Westside was built in 1922 and phased out for school use in 1967. Originally called Branch #1–Las Vegas Grammar School and later the Westside School, it was built on land donated by Helen J. Stewart to provide for the needs of local Paiute children. Members of the Nevada Band of Paiutes continue to this day to live on the land near the intersection of North Main and Washington Streets. "The Westside School is a historically and socially significant building for the black community, giving many black students their first experience with racially integrated education during the 1940s." (Warren and Mooney)

Pictured above, the new Westside School, circa 1922.

rooms, more than enough for all twelve grades. They were proved wrong a mere five years later.

While the school was named Las Vegas Grammar School and housed neighborhood elementary students, it also housed the high school, which drew students from the entire county. The high school was named Clark County High School. Seventeen students showed up for classes the first day. These numbers grew quickly to thirty-seven in 1912 and fifty-one the following year. The first graduating class in 1913 was made up of four students: Olive Lake, Leland Ronnow, Winona Earl, and Herbert Squires.

This arrangement only worked until 1916 when the Las Vegas Grammar School needed more room. Two contractors submitted bids to the County Board of Education. Both bids were higher than the $65,000 budget and were quickly rejected. Instead, the board turned to a local architect and requested he design a school that could be built for $43,000. Finally, a plan was agreed upon and a contractor was commissioned to build a separate high school for $42,500.

The new high school opened its doors on December 17, 1917. But townspeople were not impressed with the new structure. They felt too much space was given

A flu epidemic shut down the Las Vegas school in October and November 1918.

to the dramatic arts while other classrooms were hidden and inadequate. They complained that little attention was given to issues of heating and lighting. Superintendent Maude Frazier feared that the high school was unsafe and a fire risk.

In 1922, a $75,000 bond was passed to build three new school buildings. Two buildings flanked the original Las Vegas Grammar School: one for a kindergarten and the other for the domestic science program.

When a new high school was built in 1930, the upper elementary grades moved into the former high school. Four years later, on May 14, 1934, the old high school caught fire and was destroyed as predicted. The sixth, seventh, and eighth grade classes were held in tents and without plans to rebuild the school, the classes languished in tents for the next two years. The new Las Vegas Grammar School opened in 1936 at Fifth and Clark.

With continuing growth, Las Vegas added several new schools in 1943: North Ninth, Mayfair, Helen J. Stewart, North Las Vegas #2 (Jefferson), and John S. Park in 1948. And the growth continued.

Henderson Area Schools 1955

Site of Valley View School 1956
(renamed Chester Sewell ES)

Carver Park School 1943

Park Village School 1955
(renamed Robert Taylor ES)

Boulder Highway

Townsite School 1942

Basic Magnesium Plant 1942

Basic Elementary School 1953
(renamed Gordon McCaw ES)

Basic High School 1954

Henderson

In 1932, in what is now called Henderson, a one-room school sat along the railroad between Las Vegas and Boulder City. It served the area known as Texas Acres, a collection of squatters' shacks, bootleg joints, and roadhouses. Alunite, a mining stock promotion scheme from 1904–1911, brought many prospectors and mining claims, but produced little. Several families existed in the area. Since the mine didn't produce much gold, the school remained small until the early days of World War II. When magnesium was discovered near Gabbs, Nevada, President Franklin D. Roosevelt appropriated sixteen million dollars to build a magnesium processing plant near Las Vegas, as magnesium was an important mineral used in making bombs and aircraft. The nearness of the railroad as well as the availability of electrical power and water made this a particularly attractive site for the new factory.

As the Basic Magnesium Plant was being built in 1941, several small camps sprang up along Boulder Highway to accommodate workers waiting for permanent homes in the Basic Townsite. The townsite had been laid out, and soon the federal government constructed several hundred small houses and apartment complexes to house the new workers. The government quickly established a school on land that has since become the grounds of the current Henderson Civic Center. The Townsite School officially opened on October 5, 1942, with thirteen teachers

In 1943, the US Government established Carver Park, a housing area for the black workers at the magnesium plant. There were enough children that a school was necessary. A surplus Civilian Conservation Corps barracks was moved from Las Vegas and converted into six classrooms. In 1950, two rooms in the Carver Park Housing Administration Building were converted for use as classrooms for a kindergarten and a first grade class. The school closed in the early 1960s. Carver Park students moved a short distance across Lake Mead Road to Valley View Elementary School, which was later renamed in honor of Chester T. Sewell, a well-respected school board trustee who represented Henderson before and after consolidation.

Left: First boy to attend Carver Park.

and 235 students in twelve grades as part of the Railroad Pass School District. The eighteen classrooms housed the elementary school along with the high school. Fourteen students comprised the first graduating class in 1943. The Basic Townsite was officially renamed Henderson on January 10, 1944, in honor of US Senator Charles B. Henderson of Nevada and on May 24, 1946, the Railroad Pass School District became the Henderson School District.

In 1946, a personnel building at the Basic Magnesium Project was moved to the Townsite School campus and converted into eight classrooms, bringing the total number of classrooms to twenty-six.

Throughout the 1940s, other additions were made to the school to accommodate the elementary and secondary students housed on this site. But these additions were not enough to serve all of the new students pouring into Henderson; a school bond in 1953 raised enough money to begin the construction of a new high school, which was completed in 1954. In 1955, with an enrollment of 450, the building was formally dedicated and named for the Basic Magnesium Plant.

A second bond issue raised $560,000 more for a new elementary school named Park Village located in the Victory Village housing subdivision. A third

Park Village School, circa 1965.

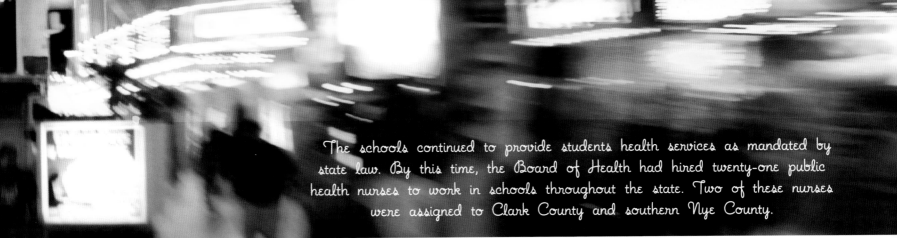

An aerial view of Hoover Dam.

Boulder City

In the fall of 1931, a housing camp was built for the workers involved in the construction of the new dam on the Colorado River on the Nevada/Arizona border. The dam itself would be the largest construction project ever undertaken by the federal government. In the end, Boulder Dam (as it was first called) was the tallest dam built in the world at the height of a sixty-story building.

As workers streamed into southern Nevada to secure jobs on the new project, the company contracted to build the dam, Six Companies, established Boulder City. Small houses and dormitories sprang up among the tents of the early arrivals. In a short time, a general store and cafeteria were established. No plans were made for a school, however.

The federal government denied Clark County and the state of Nevada the ability to tax workers and businesses located within the federal reservation. This restriction meant that the county was unable to educate the children of the Boulder Dam workers.

With no schools nearby, parents banded together to create a private school program with classes held in different homes. In September, 1931, Zella B. Larson opened up her home to eighteen first and second grade students and soon Winifred Hamilton helped out by teaching third and fourth grades in her home. Later, Harriet Gossett took the upper elementary students, creating Boulder City's first unofficial junior high. By this time, the Six Companies began donat-

grant from the Federal Security Agency funded the construction of a twelve-classroom addition to the original Townsite School campus. The expanded school housed all students until the high school students moved to a new campus in 1954. A new high school was built in 1972 and the old high school was remodeled as Burkholder Middle School.

ing residential homes to be used as classrooms. They also built a playground for the children.

As the private school program formed in these different homes, the parents agreed to pay the salary of the teachers. The parents paid five dollars tuition a month for each child along with buying their children's books. Local businesses helped out by building and donating desks and chairs.

In 1932, the federal government provided a sixteen-room school in Boulder City. The dam construction companies funded the salary of the teachers for the new school. The city manager, an employee of the Bureau of Reclamation, acted as the school board for the new school. His name was Sims Ely, and he served from October 1931 until April 1941.

The elementary district was established in 1933 when the courts finally granted the state of Nevada and Clark County the authority to tax personal property in Boulder City, and the federal government leased the building to the district, thus allowing elementary students the opportunity to attend public school for the first time in Boulder City. Sixteen teachers arrived for work the first day of classes, and their classrooms were filled with 627 elementary school students. Boulder City high school students attended classes at Las Vegas High School.

Things progressed nicely until 1938 when the construction companies moved most of their assessable wealth from Clark County and thus from the tax rolls. The result of this maneuvering was a school district facing bankruptcy. The federal government stepped in and allotted forty-five dollars per school year for each student who was the child of a federal employee living in Boulder City.

Boulder City Temporary School, circa 1932.

Railroad Pass School, 1930s.

As Boulder Dam neared completion, families moved away from Boulder City. With newly available space in the school rooms, the local school district added ninth grade in 1936 and tenth grade in 1939. When the federal government built a gymnasium and other classrooms in 1941, the Boulder City School was able to provide kindergarten through high school education.

When World War II began, the population of Boulder City rebounded and the school was soon overcrowded. The community petitioned the US Congress to provide more educational space. The War Production Board approved temporary construction

in 1942, but it was decided to delay construction until the needs of the students could be met through permanent structures. In the meantime, classes were held in church basements, army barracks, and a recreation hall.

Following World War II, the federal government began construction of a permanent junior-senior high school in Boulder City. The building was completed in 1950. The gymnasium and athletic fields were established in the intervening years. All of the funding came from the Colorado River Dam Fund.

Special Education

In the early days of education in Clark County, there were few organized services for handicapped children in the schools. Blind and deaf children had to leave the state for their education and students with other handicaps had to make do with what was available.

In 1949, parents of physically and mentally challenged children met to discuss special education. Their efforts eventually led the Nevada legislature to authorize a study in 1951, which found there was a need for special education services, though it took no action, leaving decisions to the 1953 legislature. This legislature allocated some funds to schools with special needs children allowing school districts to create smaller classes for students with special needs.

The community became a resource for the education of the physically, mentally, and emotionally challenged. In 1950, businesspeople, hotel owners, and community leaders organized the Las Vegas chapter (known as Tent 39) of the Variety Club. The club's major focus was providing funding for the education

Student and Variety Club members at the Variety School.

of handicapped children. Their fundraising efforts included a major show every year. Notable entertainers made appearances and performed at the event, which was attended by thousands of people. Enough money was raised over two years to build a school for the orthopedically handicapped.

The Variety Club donated the school to the Las Vegas Union School District in 1953. The school district, in turn, named it the Variety School for Special Education. Its first principal, Howard Marr, was noted for his visionary leadership, which was instrumental in introducing and nurturing programs on this unique campus.

Initially, the school had a staff of five certified teachers, a secretary, and a custodian. Students

Wheelchair accessible school buses made transportation easier.

Society for Crippled Children paid the salary of a physical therapist who worked out of a room at the Variety School. Henderson parents hired a private teacher to educate their special needs children. This "school" operated as a private enterprise until consolidation in 1956. At that point, the special education program became part of the school district.

Under the direction of Dr. Robert Foster, a rudimentary program was also established at the Helen J. Stewart School (now the Biltmore Continuation School), serving students with a vast array of handicapping conditions. The program eventually moved to its new site in the 1970s at the corner of Viking Road and Eastern Avenue. The school for the handicapped was named in honor of Helen J. Stewart's daughter, who was also a special needs student.

Early Technology

Educators in the 1940s and 1950s began to embrace moving film as a potential tool. It was expected to revolutionize the way schools teach and students learn. Some education visionaries thought film would replace teachers. In the Las Vegas, Henderson, and Boulder City School Districts central film-lending libraries became an important resource for teaching and staff development. Collections included 16mm instructional films, 35mm filmstrips, photo collections, and various projectors and viewers that were loaned to schools that could not afford to purchase them. Microfilm was the state of the art techology

received speech, physical, and occupational therapy. With its success, programs were added for emotionally challenged students in 1954. By 1955, the Las Vegas Union School District was the first district in Nevada to hire a school psychologist, Dr. Irving Lazar.

Other organizations also contributed to the education of handicapped children in Clark County. The Women's Service League helped pay the salaries of special education instructors and helped with the transportation of physically challenged children. The

for archiving school records. The first commercial television station in Las Vegas, KLAS–TV, Channel 8, went on the air July 22, 1953, but educational television programming, which appeared nationally in the 1950s, was not available to southern Nevada until later.

Until then, radio broadcasts were used as a teaching resource in southern Nevada, especially in the area of classical music, and current events of historical and political interest. Records and audio programs for teaching with reel-to-reel tapes gained favor among teachers as tape recorders became available.

———

Though settlers originally came to southern Nevada for agricultural, mining, or industrial opportunities, they established the foundation for what would become a community known around the world as a place of opportunity, new beginnings, and unique experiences. And just as the Las Vegas valley has grown and changed with the times, so has education. From these humble beginnings, the future fifth largest school district in the nation began to emerge.

Prior to 1955 there were almost forty school sites and more than a dozen school districts spread throughout Clark County. The disjointed approach was soon to end.

Sixteen milimeter film viewing.

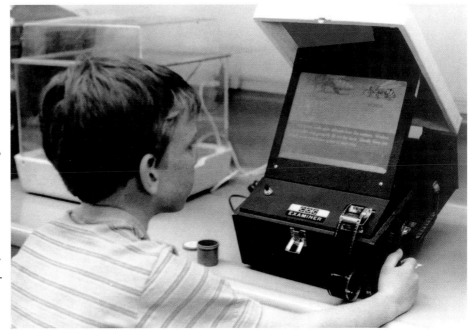

Filmstrip viewer.

Buildings used for educational purposes prior to 1955 CCSD consolidation

Las Vegas and North Las Vegas:
  Biltmore
  Bonanza ES (later named Mabel Hoggard)
  Crestwood ES
  J.C. Fremont ES (later converted to a junior high school)
  Highland (later named Kermit R. Booker)
  Jefferson (later converted to an alternative school)
  Las Vegas Grammar School (5th Street School)
  Las Vegas High School (later converted to the Las Vegas Academy of International Studies and Performing Arts)
  Lincoln ES
  Madison ES (later renamed Wendell Williams)
  Mayfair ES
  Mountain View ES
  Nellis AFB (later renamed Lomie Heard ES)
  Nelson
  North Ninth
  Paradise ES
  John S. Park ES
  Rancho HS
  J.D. Smith ES (later modified as a junior high school)
  Helen J. Stewart ES
  Sunrise Acres ES
  Twin Lakes ES
  Washington ES (later converted to Washington Continuation High School)
  West Charleston ES(later renamed Howard Wasden)
  Westside
  Whitney ES

Henderson:
  Basic ES (later renamed Gordon McCaw)
  Basic HS
  Carver Park ES
  Park Village ES (later renamed Robert Taylor)
  Townsite School
  Valley View ES (later renamed C. T. Sewell)

Boulder City:
  Boulder City ES
  Boulder City JH/SH

Moapa & Virgin Valleys:
  Bunkerville School
  Logandale School
  Mesquite School
  Moapa Valley HS
  Overton School
  Virgin Valley HS

Other County Schools:
  Blue Diamond
  Goodsprings
  Indian Springs School
  Searchlight
  Sloan School
  Variety School

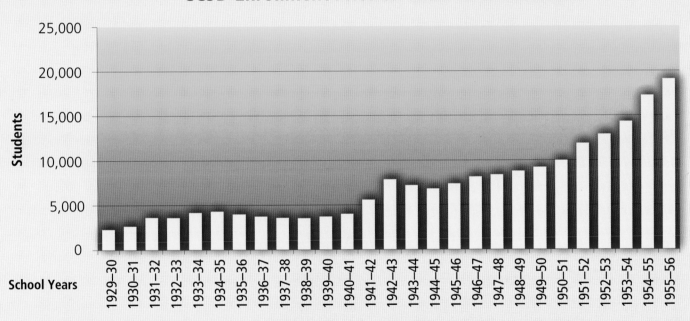

CCSD Enrollment Prior to 1956 Consolidation

A Decade of Change

- The polio vaccine, developed by Jonas Salk, was introduced to the public in 1955. Within a few short years, a disease that had crippled or killed tens of thousands of people a year nearly vanished in developing countries.

- The Soviet Union gained in power and world prominence with the launch of Sputnik 1 in 1957, spawning fears that America was slipping as a superpower. In response, the United States passed the National Defense Education Act of 1958. This act funded science and math media-based instruction in America's schools.

- In 1962, the US Congress took further action and enacted the Educational Broadcasting Facilities Program, which funded seventy-five percent of the construction and equipment of a national network of educational television stations.

- Fidel Castro overthrew the Batista regime in Cuba in 1959, seizing and redistributing land owned by American companies, and forging an alliance with the Soviet Union.

- By the early 1960s, television became a fixture in American homes. Kitchen appliances were invented that provided greater efficiency and convenience. The suburbs became the preferred neighborhoods for raising families away from the hassles and vices of large cities.

- The GI Bill made it possible for thousands of young men to go to college and gain opportunities for higher wages.

- The country was shocked by the assassination of President John F. Kennedy on November 22, 1963. The time of prosperity, the Beatles, and cultural security was being shaken as the world became less certain.

- The civil rights movement that began in the 1950s, gained momentum. In 1964, Congress passed a civil rights act forbidding discrimination on the basis of race or gender in hiring, promoting and firing, as well as denying federal aid payments to any school district that applied discriminatory practices.

CHAPTER 2

From Many, One 1955–1964

Education changes came to southern Nevada on the wings of major technological advances for the times: local electric power generators, inexpensive access to phonograph and records, moving film, radio, television, touch-tone telephones, and audio visual teaching projectors. In 1956, the newly-formed Clark County School District was positioned to take advantage of these benefits and to make great leaps forward, not only in education, but in its use of new technology in the classroom.

Clark County in the 1950s was a much different place than we see today. Las Vegas had less than fifty thousand people, though it was still the largest city in the county. To the southeast stood the industrial towns of Henderson and Boulder City, a company town that did not allow gambling and, at that time, outlawed the sale of alcohol.

To the northeast, the conservative towns in the Moapa and Virgin Valleys boasted communities that did not rely on entertainment, industry, or government projects for their existence. The residents were the descendants of the original settlers who struggled to create a stable environment for ranching, farming, and other agriculture.

A number of old mining towns also ringed the county. These communities had seen better days before 1956, but the rugged characters who worked the mines and their descendants made sure their communities survived.

When it came to education, the rugged independence of these diverse communities resulted in a rather complicated system of schools and school districts. An early state law allowed for many school districts within counties. This law gave county commissioners the authority to establish a new school district whenever their area had five or more school-aged children. Once established, the schools would be eligible for state education funds, assuming a legally qualified teacher was present in the district and the school term lasted a minimum of six months with a daily attendance average of at least three students.

The Rhythmettes

Rhythmettes

In 1949, Evelyn Stuckey, a young physical education teacher at Las Vegas High School, formed a precision dance troupe, the Rhythmettes, as a way to give young women the sense of accomplishment, camaraderie, and leadership opportunities that team sports gave to male students. Modeled after the Radio City Rockettes, the Rhythmettes program gave women the opportunity to develop confidence, discipline, and self-esteem. Community service was also an important aspect of the program.

The Rhythmettes quickly gained recognition and popularity. Within a few years, they were unofficial ambassadors for Las Vegas, giving the city a more wholesome image. The troupe appeared on national television programs such as *Wide World of Sports* and *The Ed Sullivan Show*. In 1964, the community raised money to send the Rhythmettes to the New York City World's Fair.

Over the decades, 307 young women were Rhythmettes, supporting the troupe's motto: *Perfection in performance reflects perfection in living.*

This law resulted in schools springing up throughout Nevada. Any time a mining camp opened or a group of farmers gathered together, a new school was created to capture state funds. Even after mines closed down and farming communities began transporting their children to larger schools, many of the small, rural schools and districts remained. By the 1950s, there were 173 elementary districts and thirty-five high school districts in Nevada. Clark County itself had at least fourteen school districts, several with only a single school.

Unfortunately, recognition of education in Clark County was slow in developing. The majority of state legislators represented rural communities with different needs than those of Clark County, so resources were sparsely allocated to schools in Clark County. As the Test Site developed and the casino industry took root, more people began moving to Las Vegas, yet more money was not allocated for basic education. School buildings, classrooms, even textbooks were in short supply. Often, textbooks were passed from one school to another.

The prospect of having to raise taxes in order to improve the quality of education was not a priority for the Nevada legislature. In the 1930s, business leaders in Reno pushed through a constitutional amendment that prohibited estate and inheritance taxes

Dr. R. Guild Gray.

while limiting property taxes to five cents on the dollar of assessed property valuation in hopes of attracting wealthy people from other states to move to Nevada. Gambling fees and licenses during the 1940s and 50s covered the expenses of running the state, but these funds weren't enough to cover the state's continuing educational crisis. This dance between the school districts and legislature never ends.

The lack of education funds reached a point where the Las Vegas Union District had to rely on surplus military barracks from Nellis AFB for added classroom space. Many area schools were in serious disrepair. Las Vegas Union Superintendent Dr. R. Guild Gray commented that cracks in the floors of some buildings were so wide that any pencils students dropped would be lost through the floor.

Without funds to build new schools, Las Vegas Union again resorted to double sessions, where teachers at crowded schools taught one-half of the student body in the morning and the other half in the afternoon. While this approach seemed to be a solution to overcrowding, it lessened the amount of time students spent in school each year. On double sessions, the students received 220 minutes of instruction a day instead of 300. This meant that students were spending much less time in school than students in other parts of the country.

The situation was so bad that in 1953 the Las Vegas Union School District could not balance its budget. Dr. Gray requested that the grand jury investigate the state's failure to finance public schools. In a letter he wrote to Governor Charles Russell, he said:

The several school districts in Clark County are in serious financial difficulty. Some are operating on deficit budgets at the present time. Unless something is done to alleviate the present situation we fear a breakdown of the educational system. The normal repair of buildings has been seriously neglected; there isn't sufficient money to buy books and supplies required by Nevada State Law; and substandard teachers have been employed because there aren't sufficient funds to meet the salary competition of other states. At present 44 teachers in Clark County are employed with provisional certificates.

Thanks to Gray's efforts, the state legislature began looking for a solution to the educational problems. But it couldn't arrive at a solution soon enough. In 1955, Governor Russell called a special session of the legislature to make sure the situation did not continue.

Legislature in action, Carson City, 1969.

Consolidation

The Peabody Study commissioned by the legislature recommended the consolidation of small, individual school districts into large county-wide school districts, thereby creating only one school district for each of Nevada's seventeen counties. The legislature also enacted a state sales tax to support the newly-formed school districts.

Interestingly, this recommendation may have been influenced by the work of James B. Conant, a president of Harvard University and an influential member of the NEA Education Policies Commission. His book, the *American High School Today*, advocated for large school districts and large comprehensive high schools.

Clark County Education Center, circa 1964.

All three high schools that opened during this era fit the new standard of large student populations: Western, with 2,357 students, Clark, with 2,530, and Valley, with 2,531. In addition, Clark and Valley High Schools were designed with open spaces to encourage team teaching, student collaboration, and flexible grouping, all new educational strategies aimed at closing the academic performance gap between American and Soviet students.

Innovations were implemented at Ruby Thomas Elementary School, which also opened in 1964: a unique building design, as well as special curriculum that included open classrooms, the schools without walls concept, team teaching, and collaborative teacher planning time.

The district is born

Dr. Gray, who was the superintendent of the Las Vegas Union School District before consolidation, was named superintendent of the new Clark County School District. He came with a wealth of experience, having served as the Nevada Deputy Superintendent of Public Instruction, the Superintendent of the Yerington School District, and the Curriculum Director of Contra Costa County in California.

According to the law for consolidating a county's school districts, seven school board members were

elected from the membership of the old school boards for the newly-consolidated Clark County School District. Three seats were allowed from Las Vegas. The other members came from the different communities and cultures throughout the county. Henderson and Boulder City each had a representative; Moapa and Virgin Valleys shared a seat. The final member was selected to represent the remaining rural towns.

When the Clark County School District consolidated in 1956, there was a serious shortage of school

The newly-formed board worked together to quickly establish Clark County's first realistic educational operating budget of $7.5 million.

At the time, the district had 20,240 students, 1,300 employees and teachers had a starting salary of $4,000 a year.

buildings, both in number and in physical conditions of the structures. Dr. Gray presented a twelve million dollar building program to the school board. Unfortunately, this program would have required the largest bond sale Nevada had ever seen. Dr. Gray realized that the citizens of the county were not ready for such a bond after they had just been subjected to a new sales tax. Still, Dr. Gray and the school board asked voters in Clark County to pass a $10.6 million bond for the new school district. While only fifteen percent of eligible voters turned out to

CCSD's first School Board, 1956. L–R front row: Helen Hyde, clerk; Sherwin F. Garside, President; Dr. Claire W. Woodbury, Vice President. Second row: Chester Sewell, member; Milton Keefer, member; Robert White, member; Del Robison, member.

Guidance counselors

One of the requirements to be accredited by the Northwest Association of Accredited Schools was the implementation of guidance services, which established the framework for high school counselor positions in Clark County schools. Through accreditation, standards of counseling services and job responsibilities were established, as was the ratio of 400 students to one counselor at the high school level, and 500 students to one counselor for middle schools. In the early 1950s, in response to the Sputnik challenge, the job of the high school counselor was expanded to provide vocational counseling to students, particularly to encourage students to pursue careers in math and science, in addition to monitoring student achievement toward graduation. Counseling positions were expanded to the junior high schools in the late 1950s, though the positions were only halftime in the beginning; the other half of the day they returned to teaching seventh, eighth, and ninth graders.

vote, it passed by a healthy margin. The future looked bright for the new school district.

The school board worked with Dr. James MacConnell, a consultant from Stanford University, local architects, contractors, manufactures, and suppliers to determine the most practical and economical construction design for the area. Through these meetings, CCSD created an elementary school building model that cost only $6.75 a square foot instead of the expected $8.60. This design used improved heating and ventilation systems and lowered maintenance costs. The new elementary schools also had less need for artificial lighting because they had more windows and natural light into the classrooms. All plumbing and utilities were placed above ground to make them more accessible for repairs, maintenance, and future upgrades. The partitions between the classrooms could be removed or modified as the classroom needs changed.

Anticipating more growth, the district cooperated with the City of Las Vegas to establish shared school-park playgrounds. During the school day, the parks were used by the bordering school as playgrounds and athletic fields. After school and on the weekends, the community used the parks. At some sites, the city built a swimming pool at a park and CCSD built the gymnasium and dressing rooms that would be used by students during the school day and by the community after school hours. This school-park partnership not only helped the school district keep up with growth, but it also saved taxpayers hundreds of thousands of dollars. These partnerships still exist today.

The new Clark County School District faced the challenge of educating twenty thousand children scattered across an area of eight thousand square miles and had the daunting task of bringing together the different

In 1946, there were only three hotels of note on the Las Vegas Strip: the El Rancho Vegas, the Last Frontier, and the Flamingo.
By 1960, the Desert Inn, Thunderbird, Sahara, Dunes, Tropicana, Riviera, Sands, and Stardust hotels were added. Downtown added the Pioneer Club, the HorseShoe Club, the Golden Nugget, and the Fremont hotel.

community cultures into a unified education system: the children of professional, technical workers in Boulder City; the blue-collar families of Henderson; the business owners and plant managers who worked in Henderson, but chose to reside in Las Vegas, and the small mining towns scattered along the outskirts of the county.

Plus there were the rural and agrarian communities in the outlying regions of Las Vegas. The people in Moapa and Virgin Valleys predominately belonged to The Church of Jesus Christ of Latter-day Saints and professed the values of the church. Even during the 1950s, their communities stood in stark contrast to the glamour and carefree lifestyle of Las Vegas' around-the-clock entertainment community.

In addition, there were the military and federal personnel that populated the communities around US Air Force installations at Nellis and Indian Springs. These families had different educational concerns from other families in Clark County. They often came from out of state and did not expect to remain in the county after their tours concluded. They expected their children to be educated in a manner that was competitive with other parts of the country, where they might very well be assigned next.

Madison Elementary School teacher and students.

that casinos and gambling had been prevalent in Cuba before the takeover made Las Vegas a popular and practical destination for those seeking employment. Unfortunately, their knowledge of the industry was hampered by language and culture.

The fledgling school district was unprepared for this growth; once again, there were not enough schools or funds to accommodate all of the children in the county. Schools were forced, yet again, to implement double sessions, significantly reducing the amount of instructional time given to students.

The new hotels brought prosperity for Las Vegas, but with the prosperity came a social and political dilemma that was hard to ignore: The fact that a large number of new employees coming to town were black. "Although Blacks were free to live and own businesses on the east side of town, subsequent segregation practices forced most of the minority population to relocate to the Westside." (Mooney, 2005) The influx of African American hotel workers and their families deeply impacted the schools of the Westside community.

By federal law, schools were not segregated. High school students of all races were represented in classrooms across the county, as there were only a few high schools available. Elementary schools, however, were de facto segregated, as Las Vegas casino policies and housing practices of the 1940s, 50s, and 60s discouraged integrated neighborhoods. No African American student was ever excluded from a school based on race; instead, the housing practices made it unlikely that any elementary school would have a racial mix of students. In fact, though Clark County escaped the initial mandates of

To complicate matters further, as the Cold War developed, the nuclear test site outside of Las Vegas expanded operations, hiring ten thousand employees. New casinos opened their doors, requiring thousands of workers to accommodate the flood of tourists. Neighborhoods exploded with new families.

Many of these new families were displaced Cuban refugees, fleeing from Castro's new regime. The fact

Brown v. Board of Education in 1954, the elementary schools located in the Westside neighborhood had a student body that was ninety-eight percent African American.

A newcomer arrives

Dr. Gray resigned as superintendent of the Clark County School District on September 1, 1961 to take a position as vice-president of the First Western Savings and Loan Association. During his tenure, he managed to bring the district together and handle a student population that jumped from over nineteen thousand to close to thirty thousand, as well as convince the legislature to recognize the needs of Clark County. He was instrumental in garnering community support and parental involvement, as well as handling growth and development with fiscal responsibility, establishing a model for future superintendents to follow.

Harvey N. Dondero, a senior administrator during the Gray administration, agreed to act as an interim superintendent until a replacement could be hired. His intimate knowledge of the district and its operations, and having served several superintendents during his career, helped him manage the district in its transition period. He held this position for three months until the arrival of Leland B. Newcomer, who had been recruited from Southern California and hired for the position on December 1, 1961.

The month before Newcomer took office, a special election was held to vote on a $6 million bond to build nine elementary schools and a junior high school. The bond failed, leaving the school district in a tight spot as student enrollment continued to grow at a rate of thirteen percent during 1960 and 1961.

An article in *Time* magazine noted Newcomer's arrival, as well as the fact that he was taking the helm of a school district facing tough times. Roughly half of the

Harry Dondero was originally hired for a position at Las Vegas High School in 1931.

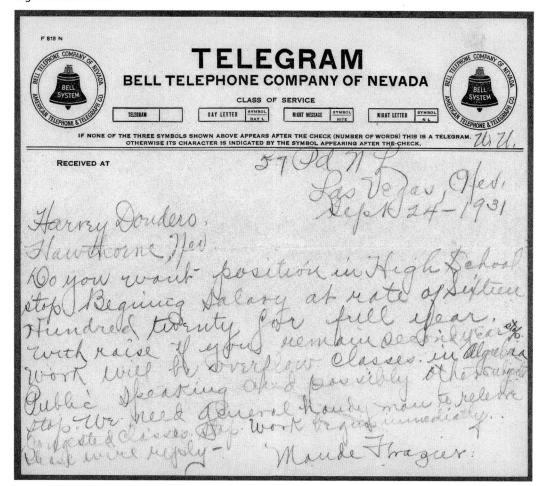

conflicts within the district, but garnered support from the community.

In fact, with the help of the PTA, a new bond issue, the largest single bond in Nevada history, was put before voters in January 1963 and passed. Yet despite its twenty-one million dollar price tag, it only provided enough funds to address two-thirds of the Clark County School District's building needs.

Left: Leland B. Newcomer.

Bus service

By 1963, the budget woes worsened for the Clark County School District. The school board worked to cut five hundred thousand dollars of the operating expenses. This reduction in expenses would have been manageable without growth, but people continued to stream into the Las Vegas Valley.

The solution was to cut various services. On August 8, 1963, the school board announced that it was ending free transportation for high school students who lived less than ten miles from school. This measure saved the school district one hundred thousand dollars .

Of course, parents and students were not happy about losing busing services. On the first day of classes in 1963, a small group of students protested the cessation of busing. They showed their displeasure by walking along Las Vegas Boulevard from the Tropicana Hotel to Las Vegas High School. Parents drove next to the students, supplying them with refreshments.

students were attending double sessions and teacher turnover was thirty-three percent.

Before Newcomer agreed to become the superintendent of the Clark County School District, he negotiated terms whereby the school board would not interfere with the day-to-day operations of the school district. Newcomer, feeling the environment was ripe for dramatic change, reorganized the district, dividing the county into five sections with a new cabinet member to oversee each area. These members acted as liaisons between the schools and the superintendent's office. The removal of the old guard with the replacement of "outsiders" caused

Student Health Services

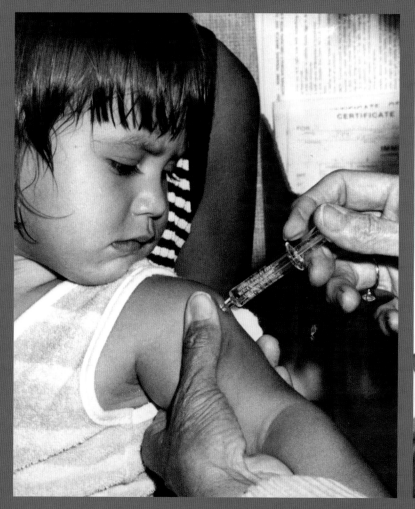

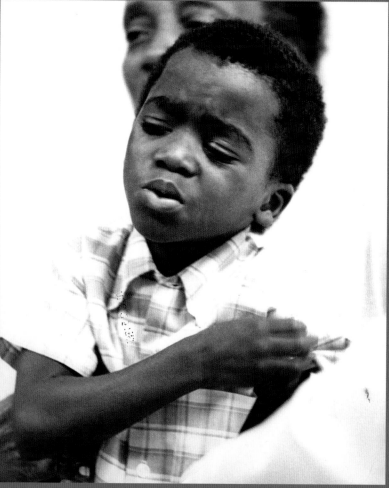

When the school districts in Clark County were consolidated, Genevieve Arensdorf was appointed to coordinate school nursing for the new district. She and her staff of five women were responsible for the health of more than twenty thousand students.

Duties included charting the height and weight of each student twice a year, checking the vision, hearing, and dental health of the students, and delivering health education. School nurses also screened children for special education.

Probably the most time-consuming duty was visiting the homes of children who had head lice. School nurses also handled tuberculin tests of food service workers and held immunization clinics.

There was no way these few school nurses could adequately complete all of the tasks and still address the health needs of individual students. Many nurses became discouraged, and the salary was not enough to keep them with the school district.

As they walked along Las Vegas Boulevard, buses partially filled with students beyond the ten-mile limit passed them, increasing the anger and frustration of the protesting students and parents. This cost-cutting measure was quickly rescinded.

To counter the shortfalls in previous budgets, Superintendent Newcomer and the

Bombs on campus

A series of bomb threats was made against junior and senior high schools in March of 1963. Protocol called for the schools to be shut down for twenty-four hours following each threat. Schools were closed on a dozen occasions.

This tactic meant a huge loss of revenue for the school district since teachers, support staff, even bus drivers were still paid during these closed days. It was estimated that each bomb threat cost $1.80 per student for every school day missed. This financial strain caused a change of policy: The city agreed to close schools only overnight following a bomb threat, returning students to classes as soon as possible.

Superintendent Newcomer also declared that students would be required to make up lost instruction time from the bomb threats. Clark County schools soon returned to normal.

Paradise and Airport, 1969.

board of trustees drew up a $26.4 million budget for the 1964–65 school year. This was a sizable increase from the $19.9 million budget for the 1963–64 year and $15.2 million the year before that (1962–63).

And so it was that the first decade of the new school district began in controversy. In a time of expansion and growth, when new ideas and fears were emerging, the fledgling school district struggled not only to deliver quality education, but also to address the concerns of the community. These themes would resurface throughout its history.

Clark High School science class..

Schools built 1955–1964

Elementary Schools:
- O. K. Adcock
- Rex Bell
- Walter Bracken
- Marion Cahlan
- Kit Carson
- Lois Craig
- Paul E. Culley
- Laura Dearing
- Ira J. Earl
- Ruth Fyfe
- E. W. Griffith
- Doris Hancock
- Fay Herron
- Halle Hewetson
- Matt Kelly
- Robert E. Lake
- Lincoln
- Jo Mackey
- J. E. Manch
- Quannah McCall
- J. T. McWilliams
- John F. Miller (later converted to a special school)
- Red Rock
- Lewis E. Rowe
- C. P. Squires
- Ruby S. Thomas
- J. M. Ullom
- Vegas Verdes
- Rose Warren
- Tom Williams

Middle Schools/Junior High Schools:
- Jim Bridger
- K. O. Knudson
- Frank F. Garside
- Robert O. Gibson
- Roy W. Martin
- Hyde Park

High Schools:
- Ed W. Clark
- Valley
- Western

Alternative/Special Schools:
- Desert Rose Adult High School

Ten Years of Social Upheaval

- President Lyndon B. Johnson signed the Elementary and Secondary Educational Act (ESEA) on April 11, 1965, passing into law one of the largest federal education laws that actually provided significant funds for kindergarten through twelfth grade programs. Originally slated to end in 1970, the act continues to be reauthorized by the US Congress. A key component of ESEA, Title I, set aside federal funds to provide services to low-income students, students with disabilities, those who have been neglected, or otherwise are at risk for failing in school. Additionally, Title III provided funds for bilingual education.

- The counter culture cycled into full swing during the late 1960s with the Summer of Love in San Francisco in 1967 and the Woodstock Festival in 1969. Free love, drugs, and rock n' roll became a theme of the hippie generation.

- At the same time, a series of assassinations rocked America. Civil rights activist Malcolm X was killed on February 21, 1965. On April 4, 1968, Martin Luther King, Jr. was gunned down. Robert F. Kennedy was assassinated a few months later on June 6, 1968.

- Civil disobedience, civil rights, and social unrest brought calls-to-arms; most notably, the riots at the 1968 Democratic National Convention in Chicago, and the National Guard shootings at Kent State University in 1970.

- On July 20, 1969, Americans gathered around their televisions to watch the lunar landing. Through grants to state and local districts, programs were implemented to accelerate math and science instruction to rival the initial technological space leap of the Soviet Union. The US Government also provided National Defense loans to support teacher training in math and science.

- The United States Congress passed an education amendment known as Title IX in 1972, which mandated that no one should be excluded from participating in educational programs based on gender. The bill's major focus was to provide school athletics programs for female students.

- The Vietnam War finally came to an end with the Paris Peace Accords on January 27, 1973. The Watergate scandal brought an end to Richard Nixon's presidency in 1974.

Striving for Equality 1965–1974

Dr. Newcomer continued to search for funding, applying for and receiving a grant from the Ford Foundation. He also put forth another bond issue and spoke before a rare joint session of the Assembly and Senate of the Nevada legislature. Newcomer believed Nevada residents wanted quality schools and wanted to be proud of their educational system and he willingly fought for them. Then suddenly in December 1965, Newcomer gave notice of his resignation to the school board. Though politics and community dissension may have contributed to his decision, it was really much simpler than that; he'd been offered a job back in southern California, on the coast, which he had always wanted.

After a nationwide search, the Clark County School Board selected Dr. James I. Mason, the current superintendent in Ithaca, New York, to replace Dr. Newcomer. Unlike Dr. Newcomer, who had never been a superintendent before, Dr. Mason had eight years of experience, having been superintendent of schools in New Jersey as well as New York.

Almost immediately, Dr. Mason faced two difficult challenges: one was growth, which had been steady, but was about to explode with the projection of significant expansion in the casino industry; and the other was the lack of ethnic diversity in the elementary schools, which contributed to racial tension and unrest in neighborhoods.

Early integration

In light of the Civil Rights Act and the threat of losing federal funds, desegregating the Las Vegas Westside schools became the more pressing issue. While the Board of School Trustees and the courts were jockeying about what to do to meet desegregation guidelines, some schools were preparing for the future. Three of these efforts were coordinated out of Jo Mackey Elementary School by Principal Dennis Ortwein: the Program of Social Enrichment (POSE), where classes from the seven African American populated schools were matched with cross-town classes for monthly social and academic activities; Volunteers for Education, headed by Edythe Katz, where classroom assistants worked in the seven schools; and the Westside School Council, chaired by Mabel Hog-

Right: An Integration Task Force meeting.

Dr. James I. Mason visits a summer school class during a visit in 1966.

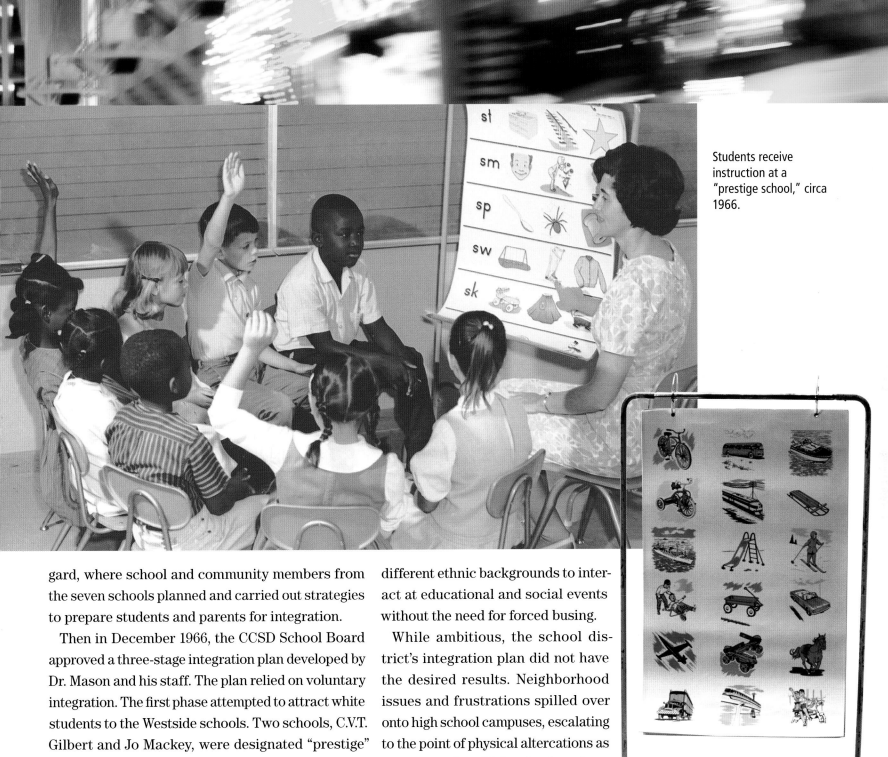

Students receive instruction at a "prestige school," circa 1966.

gard, where school and community members from the seven schools planned and carried out strategies to prepare students and parents for integration.

Then in December 1966, the CCSD School Board approved a three-stage integration plan developed by Dr. Mason and his staff. The plan relied on voluntary integration. The first phase attempted to attract white students to the Westside schools. Two schools, C.V.T. Gilbert and Jo Mackey, were designated "prestige" schools. These schools offered innovative instructional methods to attract students of all races from different parts of Las Vegas.

The integration plan also sought to attract black students to predominantly white elementary schools. The goal was to create opportunities for students of different ethnic backgrounds to interact at educational and social events without the need for forced busing.

While ambitious, the school district's integration plan did not have the desired results. Neighborhood issues and frustrations spilled over onto high school campuses, escalating to the point of physical altercations as black and white high school students fought among themselves. On several occasions, police were called to control disturbances in school parking lots. African American students also boycotted classes and staged nonvio-

Students at Fyfe Elementary School.

lent protests and sit-ins in school cafeterias.

On May 13, 1968, members of the community, as well as the League of Women Voters, joined with the NAACP to file a court complaint, known as Kelly v. Clark County School District, in an effort to curb segregation in elementary schools. The lawsuit named Superintendent James Mason and the Board of School Trustees as defendants in a case that alleged the plaintiffs' Fifth and Fourteenth Amendments rights had been violated. They said the student population in Westside schools, which was ninety-eight percent African American, were deprived of equal protection under the law. The suit claimed that black students were not getting the same education as white students in the school district.

The lawsuit also noted that there were only three African American principals in the Clark County School District, and each of them was assigned to schools in the Westside. The plaintiffs complained that black educators were not being assigned to predominantly white schools, thus limiting their career potential based on race.

As the case progressed, the plaintiffs asked Judge Roger Foley to recuse himself from the case, as he had strong connections to the power structure in the community and therefore had a potential bias. Judge Foley honored the request and stepped aside on September 23, 1968. Judge Bruce Thompson was named as his replacement and the trial date was set for October 14, 1968.

————

At the same time he was overseeing efforts at desegregation, Dr. Mason met with Howard Hughes' associates, as he recognized the school district's need to anticipate future development. Once he learned of the corporation's plans, including the Summerlin project, and calculating the number of children who would be flooding into Las Vegas with their families, the school district estimated that the student population could expand by as much as twenty-five percent in a single year.

CCSD did not have the capability to accommodate such an increase. The predictions showed consistent growth, projecting that the student population could reach as much as 93,000 by 1973.

With these numbers in hand, the Clark County School District asked for a $50.5 million bond to build twenty-two new schools and modernize existing ones. The bond passed by fifty-six percent on May 21, 1968. To make the best use of these funds, and also in an effort to save time, the school board approved architectural plans that were used to build a cluster of new schools, rather than having to go back to the drawing board for new school buildings one at a time.

Dr. Guinn appointed

Dr. Mason saw the bond issue through, and then rather abruptly turned in his resignation. Dr. Mason's assistant superintendent, Dr. Kenny C. Guinn, was appointed as Mason's successor in 1969. And though Super-intendent James I. Mason had been named in the civil rights lawsuit, newly-appointed Superintendent Guinn became responsible for implementing the plan for integrating elementary schools by April 10, 1969.

Dr. Kenny Guinn.

———

In the early days, school security was not a major issue for CCSD; teachers, student athletes, and hall monitors handled keeping the peace on school campuses. But the social pressures and activism of the late 1960s and the influx of gang activity from southern California that began in the 1970s demanded a more organized and professional approach to school security.

In 1973, in response to racial tensions and civil unrest, the Clark County School District began seriously address-ing school security concerns, designing the newest high

Student news anchors on the set of Channel 10. Below: Valley High School student gets instruction in the computer center.

school, Chaparral, so that sections of the building could be cordoned off if there were some type of unrest within the school. This design stands as a reminder of the concerns, fears, and social conflicts of the time, as well as the problems schools began to experience as Las Vegas transitioned from a small frontier town to a major city.

Educational television

As a result of the Public Broadcasting Act in 1967, which funded national programming for educational television stations, the Clark County School District received a federal equipment grant for a proposed statewide network to be based in Las Vegas with relays throughout the state. Studios and control rooms were set up in converted classrooms at the Southern Nevada Vocational-Technical Center in Henderson. For the first eight months, the Las Vegas PBS television station, Channel 10, only broadcast in the evening.

Channel 10 broadcast to Clark County classrooms for the first time on March 25, 1968. By the following October, classes

were provided via television to both elementary and secondary students. The station was one of the first truly educational stations in the nation, bringing classes to schools in rural parts of Nevada. This was an important effort, since many communities did not have the ability to fund top-notch educational programing.

Educational television upgrades to school infrastructures made closed circuit television possible for individual schools to produce in-house television shows. The same technology led to the use of videotaped feedback for teachers and students to use to watch and critique their own classroom performance.

With fewer than seventy thousand homes in Clark County at the time, Las Vegas was the smallest city to have a public television station.

The station also began airing the *Homework Hotline* program, which provided students the opportunity to get help with their homework after school from their home telephones. Students called in their questions, and volunteers at Channel 10, armed with current textbooks and reference material, would research the answers and demonstrate solutions on television for viewers. The program is still in effect.

Channel 10 cameraman, for PBS distance learning.

Students follow along with a lesson via television in the classroom.

Curriculum and Technology Changes

In the mid-1960s a controversy over reading instruction was fueled by Rudolf Flesch's book, *Why Johnny Can't Read*, which was originally published in 1955, but appeared later in a serial version in many newspapers. Similar concerns over a perception that the "new math" had led to poor math performance were encouraged by Morris Kline's, *Why Johnny Can't Add: The Failure of the New Math*. Both issues brought about a national "back to basics" movement, which may have been a factor in the Clark County School District's adoption of the Reading and Math Management Systems, used successfully in other parts of the country, to give consistency to elementary school teaching. The Management Systems called for the acquisition of scantron equipment for test scoring and data analysis software at the district level. The reform efforts also led to the creation of reading and math specialists at the district level and clerical positions in the schools to provide support and training in the management systems. By 1974, itinerant support staff positions were created to implement the Reading Improvement Program, known as RIP.

In the educational technology arena of the 1960s and 70s, eight mm film loops were added to the photography genre of learning materials. Cassette recorders were beginning to supplant reel-to-reel audio tape equipment. Programmed learning, in the form of books and multimedia kits, was another example of educational technology that gained favor in 1970s.

Educational strategies emphasized individualized student instruction, including individual and small group use of projectors, viewers, and other audio-visuals. Valley High School students and teachers were working with punch tape computer applications as early as 1968.

Volunteers provide
assistance at the
Homework Hotline.

There were 62,944 students enrolled at the beginning of the 1966-67 school year; an increase of over forty thousand students in the first ten years of the consolidated Clark County School District.

Casino Center, circa 1968.

Vocational Training

Although Nevada is one of only a few states without a budget designated to supplement the cost of career and technical education programs of study (formerly called vocational education), there were programs in domestic sciences and agriculture as early as 1913. In anticipation of the passage of the Smith Hughes Act of 1917, which provided funds to train teachers of home economics and agriculture education, State Superintendent of Education John Bray asked for and received funding from the Nevada legislature to support vocational programs.

Junior high schools built in southern Nevada in the early 1950s were designed to allow students access to introductory programs in industrial arts and home economics. High schools, like Las Vegas and Rancho, were also equipped to teach nutrition, cooking, carpentry, metals, and drafting.

In 1965, under the guidance of Ray Sturm, the Clark County School District opened its first vocational high school, the Southern Nevada Vocational-Technical Center. Special courses were offered in occupational training that were not typically available at other high schools. Students from throughout the county attended full time. Amazingly, the land for S.N.V.T.C. was purchased from the Bureau of Land Management for only one dollar an acre.

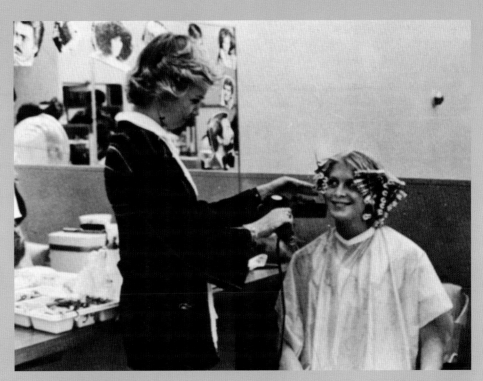

Pictured: A 1978 Cosmetology class at the Southern Nevada Vocational-Technical Center. Students learning the culinary arts at the center in 1978.

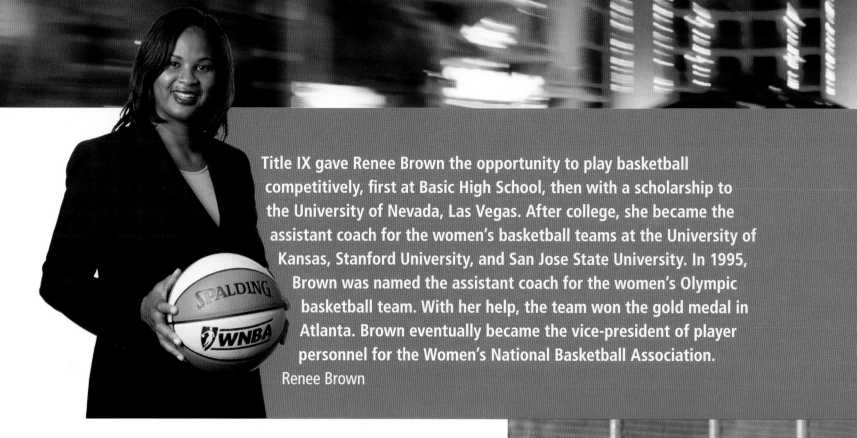

Title IX gave Renee Brown the opportunity to play basketball competitively, first at Basic High School, then with a scholarship to the University of Nevada, Las Vegas. After college, she became the assistant coach for the women's basketball teams at the University of Kansas, Stanford University, and San Jose State University. In 1995, Brown was named the assistant coach for the women's Olympic basketball team. With her help, the team won the gold medal in Atlanta. Brown eventually became the vice-president of player personnel for the Women's National Basketball Association.

Renee Brown

Title IX: Athletics programs

In the late 1960s, Las Vegas middle schools and high schools didn't have athletics programs for female students. Female sports activities were run through city recreation programs.

In 1970, Robert Lunt, head of student activities at CCSD, attended the American Health Association Conference where principals, administrators, and other educators discussed the need for equal athletic education opportunities. When Lunt returned from the conference, he advised Superintendent Kenny Guinn to prepare for changes in female sports programs.

Guinn agreed, and rather than wait until Title IX passed, he directed the district's student activities department to develop a co-educational sports program; Norm Craft and Judy Cameron were given the responsibility to make that happen. In the spring of 1971, girls' softball was chosen to be the first sport offered in CCSD schools. It was the easiest

to implement; no extra facilities were required and there were faculty willing to coach.

But a simple softball program fell short of a totally equal athletics education program. After a year-long study of programs in the rest of the country and the possibilities and limitation of schools in Clark County, the Student Activities Department presented a plan to the school board for beginning a full sports program at area high schools.

Soon golf, tennis, and basketball were added to the girls' athletics program, with track-and-field and volleyball added a year later.

By the time Title IX passed in June 1972, the Clark County School District's girls' athletics program was up and running, though there was little money to support the teams. School budgets could only cover three to four-hundred dollars per sport. This meant the coaches paid for uniforms, equipment, and even travel out of their own pockets.

Integration Plan

In December 1970, US District Judge Thompson ruled that the school district had not achieved integration through its voluntary plan. He said the neighborhood school concept needed to be abandoned to achieve racial integration. Since white parents did not voluntarily send their children to Westside schools, busing was needed to enforce integration. The final ruling was that no school should exceed

fifty percent enrollment of African American students.

Dr. Edna Hinman defined a basic plan and is credited as the principal architect of the Sixth Grade Center Program for integration. The school board authorized the plan on April 8, 1971, which was implemented the following year.

The integration plan turned the six Westside elementary schools into sixth-grade centers, sending sixth grade students from all over Clark County to the Westside. Most white sixth graders in Clark County were bused to these schools, though students

Typical integrated classroom in early 1970s.

Social change, 1972.

attending schools that had achieved the desired racial mix were exempt from leaving their neighborhood schools. Students in outlying communities, Henderson, Moapa Valley, Boulder City, and Blue Diamond, were exempt from the integration plan, not because their schools were integrated, but because it was not practical to bus those children all the way across the Las Vegas Valley for classes each day.

African American children living on the Westside attended kindergarten and sixth grade at the Sixth Grade Center schools in their neighborhood, but were bused to different parts of the district for grades one through five. White students, however, were only bused out of their neighborhoods for sixth grade. This meant that black students were bused away from home for most of their elementary experience, staying close to home in kindergarten and then

only returning to their neighborhoods for sixth grade. The inequality of this arrangement was not lost on parents, though without a more practical plan, Clark County School District had little choice but to create these sixth-grade centers.

The school district had a $1.5 million budget for its integration program. At the time, there were approximately four thousand sixth graders in Clark County and 3,300 black elementary students. Thirty new buses were needed to transport students across Las Vegas. The school district spent $540,000 on these buses and an additional $246,650 for the salaries of the 489 drivers they hired for the new routes. Even in those times, the $twenty-two thousand spent on gas and maintenance of the buses was a significant cost.

Parents on all sides of the issue objected to the plan. The group "Operation Bus Out" hired an attor-

Aerial view of the 25th Street bus yard, 1969.

ney to file a preliminary injunction against the Sixth Grade Center Plan in September 1972. The injunction argued that the desegregation plan violated the Nevada Constitution that mandated a "uniform system of common school."

The injunction was unsuccessful, but there were other forms of resistance and protest. White residents and students held marches and rallies. Others filed civil suits against the school district, claiming that it violated Nevada law that required students to attend classes near their home. Once school started, many parents boycotted classes, keeping more than sixteen thousand students from attending classes one day. The unrest caused the opening of the school year to be postponed for ten days.

Operation Bus Out continued its activities. To ensure that students who were pulled out of the sixth-grade centers continued their education, the group held classes in undisclosed locations throughout the county. Over two thousand students attended these "secret" schools. While the classes violated state law, students enjoyed an eleven-to-one student-teacher ratio. The antibusing supporters paid the teachers' salaries. Eventually, talks brought the protest to an end and students returned to CCSD schools.

In 1972, thirty-nine schools participated in the integration plan. At that time, only six schools achieved integration goals of 9.1 percent or more African American students. By 1987, thirty-eight schools were still participating in the integration plan, but there were twenty-one schools exempt from the plan because they had achieved integration goals.

School lunches

Coincidentally, busing was the catalyst for the implementation of the School Lunch Program in CCSD schools. The National School Lunch Act had been passed by Congress in 1946, but it wasn't until the voluntary integration program of the late 60s, when students were too far away to go home for lunch, that schools began delivering cold sandwiches daily from a private vendor. After a CCSD central kitchen opened during the 1971–72 school year, hot lunches became available, and in 1973, the School Breakfast Program, which had been enacted by Congress in 1966, was implemented in the district's eighty-eight schools, as studies indicated a nutritious breakfast was essential to educational success. By 1974, a warehouse was constructed that could store enough food products to handle daily food operations for the district's forty-five hundred to five thousand meals each day.

CCSD became the first school district in the nation to offer salad bars as a lunch option to its junior and senior high school students, beginning in the 1980–81 school year.

School nurses

By 1970, there were twenty-four school nurses, hardly enough to comply with the state legislature's mandates to handle their school responsibilities as well as continue to make home visits, transport students to doctor appointments, and care for the mentally and physically disabled. Nurses also had to carry all their own screening equipment from school to school. To assist with the overwhelming paperwork, CCSD school nurse, Kay Samolovitch, recruited and trained clerks, which later evolved into the First Aid Safety Assistants (FASA) positions.

In 1973, the recommendations of the National Association of School Nurses were implemented, standards that Ms. Arensdorf had been working on for nearly twenty years to establish. Certification now required nurses to have a baccalaureate degree from an accredited school of nursing, pass board exams, and receive a license from the Nevada State Board of Education.

Nurses were spread so thin that the school district knowingly violated a state law mandating every student be given a yearly physical exam. In order to comply, each nurse would have had to give ninety-four exams every day for the first two months of school. Instead, exams were given in kindergarten, first, fourth, seventh, and tenth grades. All special education students received yearly exams, but most other students did not.

An example of a box lunch from 1964.

Len Fredrick, Director of Food Services for CCSD from 1972–1980, revamped the school lunch program by bringing together what teenagers wanted — fast foods — with the responsibility of providing nutritious meals. His Fast Food Combos, approved by the USDA Food and Nutrition Services, included burgers, fries, and pizza, replaced the traditional school lunches that students threw away. His innovative program gained national attention through the publication of his book, *Fast Food Gets an "A" in School Lunch*, and has been featured on television, CBS's *60 Minutes*, the *MacNeil-Lehrer Report*, and *NBC Network News*, as well as in local and national newspapers and magazines.

A Las Vegas student throws away a traditional school lunch.

The passage of Public Law 94–142 in 1975 did not mention school nursing directly, yet the responsibility for evaluating special education students fell to school nurses. This amounted to one nurse for every 2,772 students, or one nurse for every four high schools, one nurse for every seven junior highs, one nurse for all sixth-grade centers, and one nurse for every four elementary schools.

Eventually, the Clark County School District allotted funds for one nurse for every two schools; still, it was difficult to handle all the medical issues. The student population continued to grow, as did the number of students with special needs, as more children with special needs began attending "regular" schools. To address concerns of staff and families, especially on the days a school nurse wasn't on campus, CCSD made a commitment to increase the number of FASAs district wide.

Public Law 94–142 also required structural modifications of school buildings, once again impacting district budgets. Health offices and restrooms had to be renovated for accommodations, since many of the special needs students required catheterizations, trachea suctioning, and feeding tubes.

Special Education

In the mid 1960s, the Clark County School District had established a proficient program in its education of deaf children, costing the district $1,800 a year per child. Though Title I of ESEA provided monies for students with disabilities, federal funds were not sufficient to cover all the educational needs. The Nevada Society for the Aurally Handicapped raised enough money to pay the salaries of two full-time teachers and three teacher aides for deaf students; the program was based at Ruby Thomas Elementary School in 1964 and expanded to William E. Orr Junior High School in 1965.

With the aid of Dorothy Bokelmann, a strong commitment was made to provide speech therapy, and Dr. Don Dickenson established psychological and social services for these and other special needs students. As deaf and hard-of-hearing students developed language, speech, and lip-reading skills, they were integrated into regular classrooms. Deaf children also interacted with hearing children at lunchtime, on the playground, and in the library.

A Visually Handicapped Program was also initiated, with a resource center at Ruth Fyfe Elementary School and staff available at R.O. Gibson Junior High and Western High Schools.

In the early 1970s, with expert advice and insight from Dorothy Seigle, Dr. James Williams began coordinating special education services for the school district. Dr. Williams noticed that many regular students with other special needs were not attending regular school at the time because the programs could not accommodate certain physical limitations. Instead, a program for "home bound" students

existed with itinerant teachers visiting students in homes or hospitals. To make better use of teacher time and skills, a system of telephone connection to homes and hospitals was introduced. To better meet the needs of high school students, the telephone connection was expanded under the umbrella of Las Vegas High School staff. Classes were connected over telephone lines with speakers in both home and school classrooms. An itinerant teacher visited these students on an "as need" basis. Students taking courses this way participated in the regular classes

Aurally handicapped program at Ruby Thomas Elementary School.

Second language programs

A controversy emerged regarding whether to educate children from non-English speaking families from an ELL (English Language Learner) or Bilingual perspective. The difference is two-fold: one, the ELL method offers instruction only in English, whereas Bilingual Education allows instruction in both the native language and English; and two, ELL concentrates primarily on teaching the English language, while curriculum content is the primary focus for Bilingual Education, with English language development as a secondary goal.

Several elementary schools took the Bilingual approach, as they were able to find teachers fluent in two languages, but ELL strategies predominated. Early resource centers were created at C.P. Squires Elementary School and J.D. Smith Junior High School, but as the demand increased more consultants, teachers, and aides have been hired. Many second-language specialists split their time between schools and worked with teachers on site to develop successful methods for teaching ELL.

qualifying for graduation ceremonies with Las Vegas High School.

Superintendents during this era: Leland Newcomer, 1961-1965; James Mason, 1966-1969; Kenny Guinn, 1969-1978

Year Round Schedules

Dramatic population growth was on the horizon once again and while double sessions worked on an emergency basis to alleviate overcrowding and lack of classroom space, a new strategy was needed for a long-term solution. In the 1970s, on behalf of CCSD, principal Fenton Tobler piloted a year-round schedule to meet the demands of growth at his school, Fay Herron Elementary. If successful, the plan would slow the need for an additional school by using the existing building more efficiently. On the year-round schedule, students would attend school for forty-five consecutive days, followed by fifteen days off, on staggered forty-five/fifteen schedules, so that twenty percent of the student population would be off campus at any time. The year-round concept was received favorably by the district, and while twelve-month schedules and teacher contracts have evolved over the years, the plan has flourished and is now in use in approximately eighty elementary schools in CCSD.

Fay Herron Elementary School, 1965.

Schools built 1965–1974

Elementary Schools:
Will Beckley
P. A. Diskin
William E. Ferron
C.V.T. Gilbert
Harley A. Harmon
George E. Harris
Earl B. Lundy (formerly Mount Charleston School)
Andrew Mitchell
Vail Pittman
C. C. Ronnow
Bertha Ronzone
Helen M. Smith
Myrtle Tate
Bill Y. Tomiyasu
Gene Ward
Cyril Wengert

Middle Schools:
J. Harold Brinley
James Cashman
William E. Orr
Dell H. Robison
Ed Von Tobel
C. W. Woodbury

High Schools:
Basic (new building constructed at 400 Palo Verde Drive)
Bonanza
Chaparral
Eldorado
Southern Nevada Vocational Technical-Center

Alternative/Special Schools:
Helen J. Stewart (2375 E. Viking Avenue)

Elementary students participate in a 1970 school board meeting.

Earl B. Lundy Elementary School (formerly Mount Charleston School).

CHAPTER 4

Budget Struggles 1975–1984

After almost ten years leading the Clark County School District, in March 1978, Dr. Guinn stepped down to become a vice president of Nevada Savings and Loan. During his tenure, he not only faced the challenge of desegregating the district, he developed a sound budget, reorganized the administrative divisions, and created a standardized teacher salary schedule, which recognized and rewarded advanced educational degrees and training as well as years of service.

With all of the controversy surrounding the sixth grade center integration plan, it was significant that the superintendent who followed Kenny Guinn was an African American. Assistant Superintendent to Guinn, Claude G. Perkins took office in 1978, presiding over a district of more than 86,000 students.

Almost immediately, Dr. Perkins was in the midst of controversy. He stressed stronger academics and higher standards at the secondary level, saying he would limit the variety of less substantive courses, believing that raising the expectations would improve student performance and the overall quality of education. Within a short time, he also reorganized the district's administrative offices, creating a few new top-level positions, and reassigning several others,

garnering criticism and strong reactions from school board members and administrators alike.

Dr. Perkins felt the Clark County School District was not getting fair representation with the latest federal legislation. In November 1979, he traveled to Washington, DC, with the school district's counsel, Robert Petroni, to argue that the Rehabilitation Act of 1973 and Public Law 94–142 did not address Clark County's needs. He argued that Nevada already had laws of its own protecting handicapped students and that because the federal mandates were unfunded, a heavy burden was placed on school district budgets.

In 1981, Superintendent Perkins continued his battle for funding special education. He told the Nevada Senate Finance Committee that complying

World Events of the 1970s and 80s

- The Iranian Islamic Revolution of 1979 ousted the Shah, disrupting Iranian oil production, creating worldwide panic and soaring gas prices. Long lines at US gas stations formed, contributing to the problem. It was estimated that idling in lines at gas stations consumed 150,000 barrels of oil a day. In addition, 330,000 Iranians emigrated to the US in 1978–79, with as many as one thousand Iranian families coming to Clark County.

- In 1975, Congress passed Public Law 94–142, the Education of All Handicapped Children Act to protect children with disabilities from discriminatory treatment in schools. Later strengthened and renamed the Individuals with Disabilities Education Act (IDEA), this act provided federal funds to states that developed and implemented policies assuring a free appropriate public education to all children with disabilities.

- The AIDS virus was discovered.

- The second worst hotel fire in modern United States history happened on November 21, 1980 when a fire started in a restaurant, in the MGM Grand Hotel and Casino (now Bally's Las Vegas) killing eighty-five people and injuring 650 others.

- The PacMan arcade game became a national craze; MTV (the first twenty-four-hour-a-day music television station) gave teenagers a new reason to stay inside. The Apple computer launched the Apple IIe, and VHS and Betamax vied for consumer attention.

- Of particular importance to Nevada, Atlantic City permitted gambling.

Superintendent Claude G. Perkins, 1978.

with federal mandates for special education was draining funds for the educational experience of "regular students" in Clark County classrooms. This financial dilemma remains a struggle to this day.

At the school level, Dr. Perkins reduced class sizes in the junior high schools, keeping the class sizes more in line with elementary and high school numbers, as well as encouraging greater communication between teacher and students. He also earmarked more funds for school libraries and resource teachers, believing their services were important for the improvement and strengthening of education, and raised the bar by increasing graduation requirements for Clark County students.

The Dirty Dozen

In response to a national trend, UNLV faculty member Bill Marchant and CCSD educator Nadine Nielson created a masters degree elementary counselor program, which began in 1979. Dr. Marchant worked with CSSD elementary school principal

Developmentally delayed students listening to storytime in 1982.

The Dorothy Seigle Diagnostic Center, first located on the site of the Mayfair School and later moved to the John F. Miller campus, was of immeasurable value in moving through the implementation of the Education of All Handicapped Children Act (PL 94–142).

William Moore and the Nevada State PTA to identify and secure state funding.

Seeing a need, Dr. Perkins approached CCSD educator Steve Smith who, along with Ron Ross, wrote a proposal for an elementary counseling program. A very proactive CCSD School Board approved the program and hired twelve counselors. They saw themselves as the twelve disciples, until they returned from the State Counselors Conference in Lake Tahoe, calling themselves the "dirty dozen," a take-off on the movie by the same name.

One counselor was assigned to each of the sixth grade centers. The remaining five counselors were assigned to high-need elementary schools, serving one or two schools each. Counselors dealt with issues of abuse, divorce, death, as well as bullying, anger management, school phobia, and other behavioral disorders. They worked with students individually, in small groups, and in classroom discussions, as well as conducted parent training classes and staff development activities.

Charles A. Silvestri, circa 1987.

With the success of the program, the Clark County School Board developed a "pay as you go" plan, adding a few elementary school counseling positions each year, in the hopes of eventually providing a counselor at every elementary school.

Unfortunately, only a few years later, in the early 1980s, southern Nevada saw a slower economy and many counselor positions were cut. The Dirty Dozen conducted hours of research and data collection on the successes of the counseling program. As a result, the school board made a

By the 1976 opening of school, 83,032 students were enrolled in CCSD, 20,000 more than a decade ago.

commitment to reinstate counselors who had lost their jobs through a reduction in force (RIF), though schools were not guaranteed a full-time counselor. As late as 2004–05, many schools still shared counselors at the elementary level. Only schools with more than one thousand students or those extremely at risk had one elementary counselor per school.

Perkins became increasingly unpopular with the community, teachers, and the school board. He

opposed the unionization of teachers and proposed dissolving their negotiating rights. He battled with his own school board and district administrators, as well as with the Nevada legislature. Though there were rumblings that the pressure put on him was racially motivated, when Perkins resigned in 1981, he was quick to say that race was not the issue. Instead, he admitted to a lack of political savvy.

After Perkins tendered his resignation, the CCSD Board of Trustees turned to Charles A. Silvestri, the current Associate Superintendent of Personnel Services, to step in as interim superintendent, overseeing the twenty-fourth largest district in the nation with more than eighty-seven thousand students. He accepted the assignment, but continued in his position with Personnel Services and also acted as the main negotiator between CCSD and the teachers. Within weeks, Silvestri announced that he would not seek the position permanently, citing the volatility of the position; instead, he chose to focus on maintaining as much stability as possible while the board searched for a replacement.

During Silvestri's short time in office, he did see some success, integrating the last all-black Westside school by turning it into a sixth grade center. Unfortunately, a failed bond issue disrupted Silvestri's goals of maintaining the status quo and the tax base for Nevada schools brought in less revenue than

Dr. Robert Wentz, circa 1984.

expected. Cutbacks were looming. Lack of funds and continued growth: the same old story.

Superintendent Wentz

Dr. Robert Wentz was already superintendent in St. Louis, Missouri, but expressed interest in presiding over the Clark County School District. While stable at the moment, it was preparing for explosive growth again. When he took over the superintendent duties

for Clark County School District in July of 1982, he faced major fiscal shortfalls in the millions of dollars. He was given the difficult task of cutting seven million dollars from the budget through layoffs and program eliminations.

Wentz then took a different tack toward funding new school construction. He worked with the school board to create the Pay-As-You-Go Plan. The plan called for schools to be built only when property taxes collected were sufficient to pay for new construction.

While there was initial public support for the plan, it failed. The defeat meant the school district would face serious overcrowding in the years to come.

In addition to struggling with the community over funds for school construction, Dr. Wentz was also at odds with the Clark County Teachers Association, at least in the beginning. Teachers were fighting for better pay, smaller class sizes, and improvements in hiring practices. Yet with the budget in crisis, Wentz could not support these initiatives. By 1985, though, Dr. Wentz was able to secure raises for teachers from the legislature, bringing peace to the two sides.

Innovative Curriculum

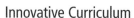

During the 1970s, Sue Morrow, the first elementary music consultant, recommended the Discipline-Based Art Education program and the Orff process she had seen at a national music conference. The Orff Music Program was introduced to CCSD elementary schools in 1975 with seventeen music specialists teaching 11,600 fourth, fifth, and sixth graders at fifty-three elementary schools. CCSD music instruction was enhanced and the first step in providing planning time for teachers was in place.

Eventually, the employment of specialists became a part of the negotiated agreement between the district and the teachers' union to provide instructional planning time for teachers during the school day.

Carl Orff, a German composer, had been dissatisfied with the quality of musicians in his orchestra, which he decided could be traced to music education in elementary school. So he traveled the world, looking for instruments that could be adapted to encourage children to become independent musicians. He created instruments with removable bars that encouraged improvisation: the glockenspiel in Germany, the xylophone in Africa, and the metallophone in the Gamelan Orchestra.

Above: Music education in practice. Right: Students perform during Orff Music Festival, 1993.

Each year, elementary school teachers donate three Saturdays a year to write, produce, and develop a music program to showcase during the annual Orff Music Festival. Some of their music has been published throughout the world. The Elementary Orff Curriculum has been presented ten times at American Orff-Schulwerk Association Conferences and Music Educators National Conferences. This curriculum has also been shared with school districts in almost every state in the US, as well as in many foreign countries. To this day, CCSD remains a model throughout the U.S. for music education.

Additionally, the School-Community Partnership Office created and organized the Class Act Program. Since 1980, this program has presented professional music performances at schools throughout the district. These programs expand the educational and cultural experience of students while reinforcing the music curriculum.

Scenes from the 1994 Orff Music Festival.

High school performing arts program.

Today there are more than 226 music specialists serving elementary schools throughout the district.

During the 1978–1979 school year, CCSD established a three-year comprehensive fine arts program that was partially funded by the federal Elementary and Secondary Educational Act (ESEA). This act contributed to professional development, instructional materials and other resources, and the promotion of parental involvement in primary and secondary education. Movement and dance were included in both the elementary music and elementary physical education curriculum in a parallel fashion. The Elementary Dance Festivals, the Regional Music Festivals, and the Elementary Music Orff Festival showcased the emphasis on music and dance.

The CCSD music program continued to grow at both the elementary and secondary levels. By 1977 there were seventy-five thousand students enrolled in music education. Band enrollment jumped twenty percent the following year and participation in the strings program doubled. Also, many private businesses pitched in to help, donating instruments and equipment.

In 1980, CCSD took over full funding responsibilities for its comprehensive fine arts program.

Also instituted during the 70s was the Academically Talented Program, later known as the Gifted and Talented Program (or GATE). The program was designed to provide support and enriched curriculum for high achieving elementary students whose needs were not being met in the regular classroom. Funding came from both the state and county coffers.

Recognition for the district's efforts in writing instruction quickly followed. The Southern Nevada

Students from Ruby Thomas Elementary School meet face to face with sheep.

Fire Safety

After the tragedy of the MGM fire, there was a general call for better fire protection in public buildings, especially in Clark County schools. Money was diverted from the new school building program to complete a fire retrofit of older schools. This process became even more costly when construction stirred up deadly asbestos dust, which had recently been linked to lung cancer and respiratory disease. The asbestos, commonly used as a fire-retardant coating in buildings throughout the 1960s, had to be removed.

Seventy-two schools had asbestos, seven of them requiring extensive and costly retrofitting. Those needing the least costly repairs were fixed first; however, complete retrofitting took twelve months for junior high schools and fifteen months for high schools. Much of the work was done after school, but some schools required a complete shutdown, sending students to attend classes on other campuses on double sessions.

Writing Project (SNWP) began in 1984 as a staff development partnership between the Clark County School District and the University of Nevada, Las Vegas (UNLV). This important collaboration involves UNLV faculty with K-12 grade teachers in an intensive summer writing workshop. Teachers learn a nationally-approved writing process while practicing, in a "hands-on" fashion, the same writing skills they will later teach their students. Teachers selected for the institute become part of an ever-growing leadership team, bringing their writing knowledge and experience back to their own classrooms, as well as providing professional development training for their colleagues. In 2004, additional Writing Institutes were added in the fall and spring to accommodate the schedule of year-round teachers.

The Southern Nevada Writing Project is affiliated with the National Writing Project which has 200 sites around the nation. It is the only federally-funded program that focuses on the teaching of writing. Teachers learn how to bring students through the writing process that includes: 1) prewriting and brainstorming, 2) writing a first draft, 3) revision and rewriting, 4) editing, and 5) publishing. The process emphasizes student choice as well as peer collaboration and sharing. Collaboration between teachers within each school and throughout the district is also promoted by the SNWP so that teachers better understand writing development across grades and subject areas. Some of the district programs for children that have evolved as a result of the SNWP include: 1) a Young Writers' Institute held in the summer, 2) a day-long Writing Fair for elementary, middle, and high school students,

and 3) the Family Writing Project — bringing family members together to write.

————

A second vocational high school, the Area Technical Trade Center, opened in 1982 in North Las Vegas. Unlike traditional vocational-technical programs, students from across the county spent half the day at their home high schools for academic coursework and the other half of the day at ATTC studying such trades as electronics and culinary arts, or preparing for careers in medicine, mechanics, and construction. Some of these classes lasted five hours in length.

In the outlying rural parts of the county, such as Moapa Valley, courses were offered in farming and husbandry, as well as programs that involved students in growing actual crops and marketing them.

The Clark County School District also developed cooperative programs with local businesses to train young people in educational and work settings. Students can obtain course credit toward graduation as they work in paying jobs. Over one thousand students work each year in retail shops, fast food restaurants, legal offices, dental clinics, and doctor offices, to name a few.

Partnership office

The Partnership office at the Clark County School District asks businesses and people in the community to work with schools. The goal is to identify community resources that can be used to enrich the educational experiences of students.

The program started in 1983 when seven businesses were partnered with seven schools. The program now has a staff of five administrators and

six support staff members. Out of this office, six hundred partnerships are arranged each year, impacting as many as forty thousand students.

The businesses and individuals inspire students to stay in school and mentor them in different profession choices. The United Way once gave the school district a five-year grant that matched adults with

failing students. The adults acted as mentors, meeting with the individual students at least once a week to make sure they didn't fall through the cracks.

Other partnerships applied the specific resources of their business to an assigned school, such as:

Sierra Health held health screenings at Twin Lakes Elementary School. They also provided crutches, wheelchairs, computers, and other equipment to the school.

Various chambers of commerce held career days and offered college scholarships for graduating high school students.

Station Casinos funding enhanced programs and facilities, such as new landscaping at C.P. Squires.

The Las Vegas Philharmonic has provided orchestral programs for thousands of elementary students in a professional concert setting.

Perhaps the most interesting and exciting partnership program is the JASON Project. Developed by Dr. Robert Ballard, the oceanographer who discovered the Titanic, the program delivers Internet and satellite broadcasts of scientific programs to students throughout the world.

Dr. Ballard started the JASON project to help middle and high school students apply math and science to real-world applications. Each year, JASON project staff develop a curriculum based on an expedition they will be taking someplace in the world. Past programs went to the Galapagos, Puerto Rico, Peru, Iceland, and Alaska. Students and teachers also have the opportunity to apply to be a part of the research team each year. Clark County students have gone to the Everglades, Belize, and were even part of an expedition that mapped the bottom of the ocean.

Schools built 1975–1984

Elementary schools:
Grant Bowler
C.H. Decker
Harvey Dondero
Elbert Edwards
Doris French
Fay Galloway
Oran Gragson
R. Guild Gray
Walter V. Long
Nate Mack

R. E. Tobler
Sandy Valley
Virgin Valley

Middle Schools:
B. Mahlon Brown
Helen C. Cannon
Elton M. Garrett
Kenny C. Guinn

High Schools:
Area Technical Trade Center

Around the Globe in Ten Years

- America officially celebrated Dr. Martin Luther King Day as a national holiday in 1986.

- The space shuttle Challenger exploded seventy-eight seconds into its launch on January 28, 1986, killing all seven astronauts aboard, including teacher Christa McAuliffe.

- The worst nuclear disaster occurred in Chernobyl, USSR, April 1986.

- Communism lost its power in the Soviet Union and the country disintegrated. The world watched as the Berlin Wall fell on November 9, 1989. Later, other communist countries also toppled, signaling a change in world politics.

- The Chinese government squashed the Tiananmen Square protests of 1989. Estimates of those killed during the massacre on June 4, 1989, range from the official Chinese reports of two hundred to three hundred people to well over two thousand dead.

- South Africa saw an end to the longstanding practice of apartheid. While racism continues to exist in the country, the release of Nelson Mandela on February 11, 1990, signaled the emergence of a new South Africa.

- Passed in 1990, the Americans with Disabilities Act went into effect in 1992, giving civil rights protections to individuals with disabilities.

- The Internet moved from an academic network to a consumer tool when Sir Tim Berners-Lee created the World Wide Web.

CHAPTER 5

Exploding Growth 1985–1994

After suffering through a long recession, things began to look up for Clark County. Homes were being built and businesses were expanding in the mid 1980s. Best of all, a young Steve Wynn announced that he was building a mega-resort the likes of which hadn't been seen in Las Vegas.

The Clark County School District had experienced a relatively steady pace of construction through its first decades, roughly two elementary schools a year. But with this mega-resort on the horizon came the promise of between three thousand and four thousand hotel workers whose children would need classrooms. Continued population growth and sharp rises in the cost of land for school sites prompted a bond election in 1984 that would fund thirteen new elementary schools. The bond failed.

This loss was a wake-up call for CCSD. Not only was the school district now short on funds at precisely the time they were needed, the school district also needed to add land acquisition to the construction budget.

The district rushed a new plan to raise forty million dollars. They proposed a 13.4 cents tax per one hundred dollars in assessed property value. These funds would still be short of the $60.1 million needed. The remaining twenty million dollars would come from excess debt reserve funds.

Since voters don't like increased taxes, the district had to sell the community on the need for additional funds. Overcrowding or deteriorating schools and the possibility of year round schools finally persuaded the community that new schools were necessary and thankfully, the new bond issue passed in December 1985.

Again, the crisis was averted, but only temporarily. More families continued to move to Las Vegas for jobs. New residents were frustrated by the lack of schools and complained loudly, especially when year-round schedules were proposed for over-crowded schools in developing parts of the valley. When a

Beckley Elementary School interior.

six hundred million dollar bond issue was proposed in 1986, voters easily approved it, funding seventy-seven new schools.

Building boom

The 1986 building program set up another "pay-as-you-go" funding that limited school construction to the taxes collected the year before. The program added $0.124 per one hundred dollars assessed valuation to property taxes; therefore, growth from new housing would pay for new school costs.

Within just a few years, Dr. Wentz faced the enormous growth he had anticipated. Two major housing developers broke ground on new communities in southern Nevada, and the new mega-resort concept began to take shape as well. With the impending opening of the Mirage Resort and Casino, families moved into Las Vegas in record numbers, surpassing CCSD enrollment projections.

The 1986-87 year opened with 91,446 students enrolled in CCSD schools.

The Mirage Hotel and Casino opened in 1989 and within months, the Mirage became the most visited tourist attraction in Nevada, surpassing the Hoover Dam in popularity.

By the opening of school in August 1987, there were over one hundred thousand students.

In particular, an increasing number of Hispanics came to the valley to fill the service, construction, and hospitality industry positions. This migration changed the dynamics of the school population dramatically. The number of students with English as their second language created additional challenges for the district. Unfortunately, the "pay-as-you-go" program involved a lag time of several years, causing a serious school shortage while the school district waited for more funds to become available.

A new bond was proposed and passed in 1988. The bond issue sought to remedy the shortfall in classroom space in Clark County; however, problems with planning models and spikes in construction costs caused CCSD to default on the number of new schools it promised. While the bond issue promised eighty-eight schools, only seventy-seven schools were built.

The shortfall resulted from the fact that when planners were putting together the budget for the 1988 bond, the builders were asked to give them the price of the last middle school built in Clark County. As usual, the planners took this number and multiplied it by the expected increase in building costs and then applied that number to the schools they needed to build.

While the information the builders presented for the last middle school built was accurate, as it turned out, the last middle school built was Garrett Middle School, a relatively small school in Boulder City. The costs were woefully under projected.

The situation was made worse by an unfriendly bidding climate and increased construction costs. For instance, new heating and air conditioning systems promised better performance and lower maintenance but cost more than older systems. Plus, CCSD found itself competing with the major casinos and developers for construction companies, workers, and suppliers in the Las Vegas building boom.

The Americans with Disabilities Act (ADA) also added to the cost of new school buildings. When the planners calculated the costs of new schools, they did not, nor could they, anticipate the new requirements the ADA required. Many of these requirements were costly and required changes to the design of the new schools.

Above: Students at Beckley Elementary School, and below at McWilliams Elementary School.

PEPCON Fire Disaster

Few people living in Clark County were aware that a dangerous substance was being produced within miles of their homes. Since 1972, the PEPCON plant in Henderson was one of only two places in the United States where ammonium perchlorate — a solid rocket fuel — was mass-produced for NASA. The other was Kerr-McGee, located less than one-and-a-half miles away.

On May 4, 1988, a series of explosions ripped through the PEPCON plant. The blast also destroyed the nearby Kidd Marshmallow plant.

Lunch had just ended at nearby schools; students were returning to their studies. When the shock-waves rippled through the schools, students panicked and teachers rushed to control the situation. Windows were blown out of classrooms as far as fifteen miles away from the location of the blast.

At the moment of crisis, the communications network broke down. The schools couldn't call out to get information from school district administrative offices. Parents calling the schools to inquire about the safety of their children were not able to get through. The television became the only source of news.

In the end, there was over eighty-one million dollars in damage to the processing plant, valley schools, and the community. The National Guard was called in to impose an eight p.m. curfew after Governor Richard Bryan declared a state of emergency in Henderson.

Amazingly, only two people, both Pepcon employees, died in the explosion and no children were seriously injured.

Following the explosion and its aftermath, the Clark County School District reviewed its emergency management strategies that had obviously failed during the crisis. Communication links to and from the schools were upgraded and intercoms were installed in schools. Principals and key staff were given two-way radios to ensure that communication stayed intact between the office and senior staff in the event of a major incident.

In addition, a new "Shelter in Place" safety procedure was implemented throughout the district. In contrast to "fire drill" procedures where students evacuate the building, students "shelter" inside the buildings and staff secures the outside perimeters.

In addition, technology took a major leap at the end of the 1980s. Classroom computers called for a technological infrastructure that did not exist at the beginning of the decade. While this technology promised efficiency and cost savings, the initial cost for the new equipment was often significant.

The passage of the federal Carl D. Perkins Applied and Technical Education Act of 1984, however, did provide additional resources to expand and enhance career training and placed an emphasis on serving students with special needs. During the early 1990s, the Nevada legislature appropriated funds designated to support new courses at the middle school level in Home and Career Skills Education and Introduction to Technology. At the high school level Clark County's Facility Division designed schools to offer students programs in automotive, business and marketing, carpentry, foods, child development, and clothing.

With funding from the federal School-To-Work Opportunities Act of 1994, funds were available to re-emphasize career awareness, work-based learning and academic integration. Partnerships with apprenticeship programs and higher education were promoted with governance from local advisory committees made up of fifty percent or more business and industry representatives.

Other problems arose, making construction more difficult and more costly. The Clark County School District was two years into the 1988 building program when the desert tortoise was declared endangered. If a tortoise was spotted at a building site, construction had to stop. Officials needed to move the tortoise before construction could resume. To solve the problem, CCSD worked with the BLM and the

Computer center at Hyde Park Middle School.

Tortoise Group, organizing an adoption policy that removed tortoises from construction sites to wildlife habitats and school habitats, as well as to the homes of animal advocates. Many tortoises were adopted by public-spirited Las Vegas families.

In total, the increased costs due to land acquisition, construction costs, as well as safety and environmental considerations accounted for fifty-five million dollars, or the equivalent of ten elementary schools. Officials were quick to point out that while they didn't build the promised number of schools, they did create the

The disasters of the MGM fire, the Pepcon explosion, and ongoing campus security concerns brought about the demand for improved communications, particularly with the use of two-way radios at individual schools and mobile phones for central administrators.

same number of seats. But the public focused on the fact that the bond did not create the number of schools promised.

An election of new trustees in 1988 changed the makeup of the CCSD school board, and the writing was on the wall. Dr. Wentz resigned as of May 1, 1989.

Superintendent Cram

Brian Cram was appointed superintendent in 1989 and like Charles Silvestri, Dr. Cram came up through the ranks of the Clark County School District. He took office just as growth accelerated in the Las Vegas Valley and became known as "the Bond Man," or the poster-boy for school bonds throughout the nation. During his tenure, Cram secured billions of dollars to build one hundred new schools in Clark County.

To challenge Dr. Cram even further, the Nevada legislature enacted the Class-Size Reduction (CSR) Act in 1989. The measure was designed to reduce the pupil-teacher ratio in the public schools for kindergarten through third grade. Though educators and parents were positive in their attitudes toward class-size reduction and fewer special education referrals were reported in initial evaluations, there is still a debate over the long-term benefits of reduced class size.

In addition, CSR's impact on education budgets continues to be a bone of contention in requests for state funds. Legislators argue that if districts didn't

Dr. Brian Cram.

insist on reduced class size, more funds would be available for salaries, supplies, and equipment.

Prime 6

As late as 1992, school desegregation continued to be an issue. Superintendent Cram established the Educational Opportunities Committee (EOC) to make recommendations for improvement to the current plan. Westside parents were still unhappy with the Sixth Grade Center Plan and continued to protest the unequal burden placed on their children. With the help of the NAACP, parents created an action group known as WAAK-UP for Westside Action Alliance Korps-Uplifting People. When the 1992 school year began, many African American parents kept their children home in an effort to prevent the school district from receiving full funding from the state. Nearly three hundred children boycotted classes, demanding an equal burden in Clark County School District's integration plan. Since state funding is based on enrollment by a specific date in the fall, this action cost the Clark County School District more than one million dollars in state funding.

On September 23, 1992, the CCSD Board of School Trustees approved a new plan that phased out the sixth grade centers, and instead, established Prime 6 schools that provided innovative educational programs with a multicultural focus and extended

Propelled by a belief that improving our public schools was too big a task for a school district to undertake alone, Ernest A. Becker, Jr., Ann Lynch, Karen S. Galatz, former governor Grant Sawyer, Dr. Lois Tarkanian, and Judi Steele established the Public Education Foundation in 1991 as an independent 501(c)(3) non-profit Nevada corporation. Their first order of business was to provide solutions to the challenges of educating a growing and diverse Southern Nevada population.

The mission of the Foundation was to mobilize community and global resources to support and impact public education through initiatives, programs, and promising practices designed to improve student performance and advance quality educational opportunities for all children. Since its inception, the Foundation has raised more than fifty-five million dollars to improve teaching and learning in southern Nevada.

The InterAct™ Online Learning Community was launched by the Foundation in 1992 to build and enhance online communication, collaboration, and knowledge-sharing by faculty, students, and administrators within the Clark County School District. Seeded by a generous donation from The Lincy Foundation and starting with a pilot group of ten schools and 300 users, InterAct™ has grown to include all schools and services within the Clark County School District. InterAct™ currently provides 11,500 students and almost thirty-nine thousand teachers, administrators, and staff with advanced email capabilities along with a comprehensive set of document sharing and social networking tools within a secure, managed environment. More than 10.5 million messages are transmitted each month and 325 school conferences are active. The system is managed by system administrators and technicians within the CCSD. The Foundation continues to pay the annual licensing fees.

The Grant Program, also initiated in 1992, offers teachers and administrators opportunities to implement best practices or test new teaching methodologies. More than $1.9 million in grants have been awarded to teachers and schools through the Foundation.

A generous donation from Smith's Food & Drug in 1995 marked the beginning of the the Public Education Foundation's Scholarship Program. The program grows

Students enjoying books as part of Clark County Reads program.

each year as a result of corporations, individuals, organizations, and private foundations, whose endowments provide funding for students to continue their education. In many cases, the scholarships make the college and university experience accessible to students who might not otherwise dream of a college education. The Foundation now offers more than ninety different scholarship opportunities for high school seniors to attend both in-state and out-of-state schools. More than eighteen hundred scholarships have been awarded, totaling nearly $4.2 million.

Launched in May 2001, the Public Education Foundation's literacy initiative Clark County READS promotes the importance of literacy and provides quality literacy programs to children and families in Clark County: the Reading Partner Program, Library Enhancement Program, Reading is Fundamental, Book Re-use Program, Boots Up For Reading, Reach Out and Read, and Ruegy's Readers. Since inception, Clark County READS has placed more than seventy thousand new non-fiction books into eighty-three school libraries, more than one hundred fifty thousand students have received five hundred thousand books, and almost sixteen hundred reading volunteers have been trained and placed in one hundred twenty schools.

Cast members from the show *Jubilee!* read to students during Nevada Reading Week.

instructional time. The new plan gave first, second, and third graders from the Westside the option of either attending one of these Prime 6 schools or a school designated outside their neighborhood. In subsequent years, fourth and fifth graders were given the same options. Students living outside West Las Vegas were given the opportunity to attend their assigned school or one of the Prime schools.

In addition, one of the former sixth grade center schools, Mabel Hoggard, was converted to a magnet school. The school offered innovative and specialized educational programs in math, science, technology, and the environment in an effort to continue promoting integration by attracting students from all parts of Clark County. Students applied and were selected by lottery. Subsequently, two other sixth grade center schools, C.V.T. Gilbert and Jo Mackey, were designated magnet schools, and later, Walter Bracken and the Sandy Miller Elementary Schools became part of the magnet school program. As these students moved through the elementary magnet

CCSD High School Academies and Institutes:

Advanced Technology Academy; Basic High School Institute of Law, Justice, and Public Service and Institute of Health, Wellness, and Medical Technologies; Canyon Springs Leadership and Law Preparatory Academy; Clark High School Academy of Math, Science & Applied Technology (AMSAT), Academy of Finance (AOF) and Teacher Education Academy of Clark High (TEACH); Desert Pines Academy of Information Technology and Academy of Communications; Las Vegas Academy of International Studies and Performing and Visual Arts; Rancho High School Aviation and Medical Academies; Valley High School Academy of Travel and Tourism and International Baccalaureate Program.

schools, programs were established at K.O. Knudsen and Hyde Park Middle Schools, and soon academies and institutes of specialized programs were developed at many area comprehensive high schools to

continue providing academically enriched education and encourage ethnic diversity.

Although racial and social equality have not been reached in society in general and Clark County specifically, the school district continues to find new ways to address educational equality.

The first school-based health clinics opened in the 1990s to provide primary care to students who attended the school where the clinic was based, as well as to their siblings and parents. In addition to immunizations, the clinics offered general health services at free or reduced costs, making medical care affordable and accessible, reducing student absenteeism.

abled and regular schools. Disabled students were given more opportunities to participate with non-disabled students according to their abilities. Even severely disabled students visited regular classrooms for an hour or so a day.

On the twenty-fifth anniversary of the Education for All Handicapped Children Act of 1975, the law was amended to become the

IDEA

In 1993, the concept of inclusion came to the forefront of education. Early successes were achieved with small-scale efforts to place severely disabled students in regular school classrooms.

The issues drew more attention when the Clark County School District settled with the Office of Civil Rights in the US Justice Department in 1993. As part of this settlement, the school district forged more partnerships between schools for the dis-

Individuals with Disabilities Education Act (IDEA). The new law stipulated that special needs children should be educated in the least-restrictive environments. The result of the act was students who were once placed in special schools were moved into their neighborhood schools. If the student needed a treatment, the procedure had to be done at the neighborhood schools.

Hyde Park Middle School students.

McWilliams Elementary School students.

Unfortunately, the new special education amendments came with no new funds and the costs of fulfilling the mandates of IDEA became a financial strain on school district operating budgets. In the 1990s, an average of forty-two million dollars a year had to be diverted from the general fund to subsidize federal special education mandates.

———

In 1994, the Clark County School District presented a new bond issue in two parts. Part A issued $605 million: $345 million for twenty-four new schools and expanding the capacity of three more schools, another $230 million for the repair of older schools, and the final thirty million dollars to buy land for future schools. Part A of the bond issue did not increase property taxes.

Part B, on the other hand, would have increased the property tax rate by 11.2 cents per one hundred dollars assessed valuation of property. That amounted to roughly thirty-nine dollars per year for a one hundred thousand dollar home (such homes did exist in Las Vegas in 1994). Part B would have issued an additional three hundred million: $180 million for building thirteen new schools, and $120 million for repairing older schools.

While voters voted overwhelmingly for Part A, Part B failed to pass by only 746 votes, or 0.3 percent of the total vote.

As people continued to move to Las Vegas, the Clark County School District had to anticipate where housing developments would be built in the desert, and begin building schools even before the neighborhoods existed. Often, developers would wait for construction to begin on a school, letting the school district pay for the infrastructure to be laid through uninhabited land, sometime miles into the desert. Once electrical, water, and sewer were in place, developers could build around the new schools at a fraction of the development costs.

The district complained about the practice and eventually an agreement called "refunding" was established. Under the agreement, when developers began construction, they would pay a fee that reimbursed CCSD for the infrastructure it had already put in place.

Master-planned communities became popular in the Las Vegas Valley, and the school district began working with developers, convincing them that they would benefit from having schools in their communities. Eventually, some developers contributed to

building costs by bringing utilities to the schools, or offering free or reduced prices of land.

Land for schools was acquired in a variety of ways: through the Bureau of Land Management, which controlled much of Nevada, eminent domain, and more recently, housing developers.

The Clark County School District faced a land crisis when the policies dictating the use of BLM land in southern Nevada changed. The federal government decided to sell BLM land to raise money for the purchase of land in other areas. This not only meant that Clark County School District now had to purchase land that was previously free, it also meant that it often competed with developers for parcels and price.

Fortunately, planners at CCSD were forward thinking. They anticipated a land shortage and set aside or purchased land well in advance of development. Without this land, the school district could not have made it from the 1988 bond issue through the 1998 bond issue.

MASE

With the introduction of the new National Math Standards from the National Council of Teachers of Math (NCTM) in 1989, a shift began both nationally and

Clark County *high* schools are usually given names that reflect the desert or southwestern characteristics such as, Desert Pines, Mojave, and Chaparral, though occasionally high school names reflect patriotism in the current political climate, like Liberty and Cimarron-Memorial. Elementary and middle schools are named after prominent individuals: community leaders, historical and political figures, or noted educators who worked for the Clark County School District, contributed to the pursuit of education, or in some cases, lost their lives in service to education.

locally in how mathematics would be taught. The new focus was on how children learn mathematics — how they find a deeper level of mathematical understanding of content and processes, including number and problem solving, beyond drill and practice and memorization of algorithms. From 1991–1995, the CCSD Elementary Division hired five Teachers on Special Assignment (TOSAs) using IKE funds (Dwight D. Eisenhower Math and Science Education Act) to provide professional development in math and science directly to teachers in their schools.

In 1992, the first of three MASE (Math and Science Enhancement) projects was being developed under the direction of Linda Gregg, elementary math

Scenes from William McCool Science Center at Lamping Elementary School named in honor of Space Shuttle Columbia Commander, who died on February 1, 2003.

In Memoriam

Students of Southern Nevada Vocational-Technical School paid tribute to the *Challenger* astronauts in their yearbook of 1986.

From the Children of the *Challenger* Crew

All at once it was done
it happened too fast,
not a word could be said
then it was over and past.
But we love you so much
it can't be true,
how are we to react
what are we to do?
We were so excited
when you left the ground
and in a matter of seconds
you were nowhere to be found
You would have been heroes
after your magnificent flight
now you're only a memory
when we go to sleep at night
You have given us hope to continue on,
and a dream to succeed
for you because you're gone
We love you forever
and wish you were here,
we will keep you in our hearts
because we know you're near.

Jeanna Cochneuer, Class of 1988

As we watched it go high
No one in its presence gave a sigh.
Then the strangest thing went on
For it happened when it started going around.
The tragedy happened right before our eyes.
It filled our minds with many whys.
We'll all have feelings for the seven
When we think of them reaching for heaven.

Rick Cobb, Class of 1988

Seven Lives of the *Challenger*

Many spectators looked on with high hopes
As the *Challenger* left the ports
Then as fear filled everyone's eyes
A large flame filled the skies
Then to everyone's surprise
The sky had taken seven lives
The seven who were making history
Whose deaths are now a mystery
So as we go on with our lives
Think of the tragedy that happened that one might
Give them the credit that they deserve
Because we know they will never return.

Stacey Holiman, Class of 1987

The shuttle disappeared in smoke
I stiffened and felt sad,
I wondered how the students felt,
They must have felt real bad
I hope they find out what went wrong,
what caused this tragedy,
and in the future I can hope
to build a ship for me!

Eric Amblad, Class of 1994

and science coordinator for CCSD. These projects were funded with grants from the National Science Foundation (NSF) for the purpose of: 1) providing extensive professional development for teachers in math and science, 2) giving teachers time to interact and learn with their colleagues and nationally recognized experts in the field of math and science, and 3) building a team of teacher leaders within the school district and at each school to carry on further teacher training. MASE I served the district until 1995, MASE II from 1995–2002, and MASE III, which included a technology component, from 2000–2006. Under these MASE projects, teachers were required to participate in one hundred hours or more of professional development. During its entirety, MASE provided training for over 8,200 educators who participated in 396,000 hours of professional development. Grant awards totaling more than eleven

million dollars were received from NSF to fund the three MASE projects.

The CCSD program put teachers and students in touch with people who made a living in the sciences. This gave a real-life perspective to science education. Students also had the opportunity to talk with the engineers designing and building the rollercoasters at Circus Circus casino, certainly a unique experience not readily available in other parts of the country.

When the grant ended five years later, the Clark County School District received an unprecedented two-year extension of the grant. By giving CCSD an extension that no other school district received, federal grantors acknowledged the success and effectiveness of CCSD's program.

The benefits of the program expanded well beyond the schools initially involved. With the explosive

In 1995, Library Services and CCSD Network Services realized there was a need for all school libraries to be maintained on a single district-wide system. The library software, Destiny, provides a truly unified catalog, keeping all circulation records in one location, equalizing access to materials for students at small, rural schools as well as larger, urban schools, transferring individual student records with the students throughout their years in CCSD. In addition, online research databases provide 24/7 access to information to students and faculty.

growth that characterizes the school district, core teachers moved to other schools, taking with them their experiences that were so successful in the original program. As time passed, many of the original teachers also achieved key leadership positions within the school district.

The Federal School-To-Work Opportunities Act of 1994 also made funds available to re-emphasize career awareness, work-based learning and academic integration in CCSD high schools. Partnerships with apprenticeship programs and higher education were promoted with governance from local advisory committees comprised of fifty percent or more business and industry representatives.

––––––

In the early 1980s, a small group of CCSD teachers were pioneers in the district's computer movement. They were among the first area teachers to attend conferences and workshops to learn the potential of computers from the likes of MIT's Seymour Papert. Later, the "pay as you go plan" funded the purchase of IBM PCs for schools to begin digital management of their library collections, and the IBM Corporation donated an additional ninety PCs for this purpose. Apple and IBM were eager to get their wares into action in the big market that the CCSD represented. Soon CCSD collaborated with the Minnesota Educational Computing Consortium (MECC) to provide virtually free access to tons of software to teachers and their students.

Computer technology

Standardization became a key issue; whether all schools should be required to use the same platform and same networking software/hardware, or if schools could be allowed to choose the platform they wished. Questions also arose whether or not networks could accommodate a mixture of Mac (Apple) and IBM types of equipment. In the 1990s, the district created a new division and hired a chief technology officer to oversee the use of technology and facilitate the resolution to these issues throughout the county.

CCSD also added itinerant computer technology specialists to its staffing model, which dramatically advanced the cause of computer users in the district. The new specialists trained teachers and students in the use of computers and related technology. They oversaw the ordering of equipment and kept existing hardware up and running. They advised principals on long-term planning and the integration of technology and curriculum. And by 1995, Interact provided online technology training throughout the district.

With their ease of use and quick retrieval of information, pictures, or sequence of events, CDs began replacing floppy disks, audio cassettes, video tape and film, eventually prompting the CCSD to do away with its film library and equipment lending service. Channel 10 now maintains a lending library of instructional programs on CD and DVD.

Schools built 1985–1994

Elementary Schools:

Kirk Adams
Lee Antonello
Selma F. Bartlett
John R. Beatty
Patricia A. Bendorf
William G. Bennett
Lucile Bruner
M.J. Christensen
Clyde C. Cox
David M. Cox
Cynthia Cunningham
Jack Dailey
Herbert A. Derfelt
Ruthie Deskin
John Dooley
Marion B. Earl
Dorothy Eisenberg
H.P. Fitzgerald
Lilly & Wing Fong
James Gibson
Helen Herr
Charlotte Hill
Edna F. Hinman
Walter Jacobson
Helen Jydstrup
Marc Kahre
Edith & Lloyd Katz
Frank Kim

Martha P. King
Martin Luther King, Jr.
Zel & Mary Lowman
William Lummis
Robert Lunt
Ann Lynch
Ernest May
Estes M. McDoniel
James B. McMillan
John F. Mendoza
Ulis Newton
Claude & Stella Parson
Ute Perkins
Clarence Piggott
Doris M. Reed
Harry Reid
Richard Rundle
H.M. Stanford
Jim Thorpe
Harriet Treem
Whitney
Gwendolyn Woolley
Elaine Wynn
Louis Wiener, Jr.

Middle Schools:

Ernest Becker
Hank & Barbara Greenspun
Walter Johnson
Mike O'Callahan

Grant Sawyer
Theron L. Swainston
Thurman White

High Schools:

Advanced Technologies Academy
Cheyenne
Cimarron Memorial
Durango
Green Valley
Las Vegas (new building at new site)
Laughlin JH/SH
Moapa Valley (new building)
Silverado
Virgin Valley (new building)

Alternative/Special Schools:

Horizon/Sunset-Burk Campus

Turn of Century Brings Uncertainty

- Terrorism came to American consciousness in 1995 when Timothy McVeigh bombed the Alfred P. Murrah Federal Building in Oklahoma City on April 19. The attack killed 168 and injured 800 others, making it the deadliest act of terrorism on United States soil to date.

- The Centennial Olympic Park in Atlanta, Georgia was bombed on July 27, 1996, during the summer games.

- The Columbine High School massacre drew the country's attention on April 20, 1999, when two students went on a shooting rampage at their high school, killing twelve students and teachers, wounding twenty-three others, and then killing themselves.

- Coined the Y2K scare, many feared great catastrophes would occur when two-digit computer "clocks" turned from year 99 to 00. Code for critical systems was quickly re-written ensuring a nearly seamless transition. The Y2K scare demonstrated society's dependence on technology.

- These events were overshadowed by the horror of September 11, 2001.

- Cable modems and DSL lines replaced less efficient telephone lines. Cell phones went from being a rare luxury to a necessity. Floppy discs were traded for CDs, and DVDs replaced VHS cassettes. Wireless technology gave consumers the ability to stay in contact with home and office at all times.

- The No Child Left Behind Act of 2001 was an unfunded mandate designed to increase the standards of educational accountability, setting the same achievement goals for all ethnic, special education, socio-economic and language subgroups within each school.

CHAPTER 6

A New Century 1995–2005

Moving into the twenty-first century, the Clark County School District had the challenge of providing safety and security on school campuses in addition to continuing to struggle with thousands of new students and not enough classrooms.

Learning from the weaknesses in security during the shootings at Columbine High School, the Clark County School District improved communications with all law enforcement agencies and emergency services. School police went through active police officer training to be prepared to respond quickly and began working with psychological services to identify possible problems before they became more serious situations.

The CCSD police department also became involved with the design of new school buildings and the remodeling of existing ones; in particular, changing the doors to older classrooms that could not be locked from the inside, meaning teachers could not protect their students from any trouble that might be happening outside the classroom. The officers also recommended the removal of large bushes from around windows and doors, as well as ways of preventing students from climbing fences to get on the roofs of schools.

Today, the department has 145 police officers supported by a staff of twenty-five full-time employees. Officers not only have radios, they also have satellite phones, and their cars have GPS locators.

The CCSD police department even has specialty vehicles, such as the thirty-foot mobile command post. All of these vehicles have direct TV capability. The Corporation for Public Broadcasting even designates a portion of its television signal for broadcasting important information directly to the officers' cars. If a catastrophe occurs, the airwaves can broadcast critical information such as building

Channel 10: The Ed-YouTube

In 1995, Channel 10 expanded programming from four to twelve educational television channels. Foreign language instruction was delivered to rural Nevada where there were not enough students to support foreign language teachers. In 1996, the Distance Education Program began offering broadcast and video courses through Channel 10 to credit-deficient students throughout the Las Vegas Valley to help them earn their high school diplomas.

Channel 10 also offers employee training classes, professional development courses for teachers, and weekly police briefings. More than 1,000 teachers have enrolled in continuing education and online certification courses. The educational media center at Channel 10 acquires, duplicates, and distributes more than one hundred thousand educational DVDs, video tapes, and CDs to Clark County schools each year.

Officially renamed Vegas PBS, Channel 10 continues to develop technology to serve the educational needs of Clark County and the state of Nevada. Vegas PBS began a curriculum-indexed educational video-on-demand streaming service to the schools in Clark County. There are more than fifty thousand videos, forty thousand images, and twenty thousand pages of teacher guides, student worksheets, and tests that are instantly accessible over the system.

floor plans, student rosters, and other critical information. As of this writing, this system is not used anywhere else in the country.

The monies from the 1994 bond were not enough to keep up with the growth; the district had to quickly begin work on the next bond issue. By the opening of the 1996–97 school year, 166,788 students were enrolled, an increase of more than seventy-five thousand students over the previous ten-year period.

While they had trepidation presenting the public with a new bond issue a mere two years after a disappointing defeat, CCSD made the public aware that the number of school buildings were not keeping up with the number of students moving to Clark County with their families. Voters approved the 1996 bond issue with close to sixty-one percent of the vote, which provided $643 million for building sixteen new schools, adding 95 classrooms, completing 275 modernizing projects, and installing 3,474 new computers in existing schools.

Also in 1996, CCSD embarked upon a venture with the Community College of Southern Nevada (now called the College of Southern Nevada). The collaboration allowed high school juniors and seniors the opportunity to take their required high school courses and college elective courses on one of the

We Know About Mass Transit   CCSD bus driver.

Demand for transportation services never waned, either. When schools went on double sessions, when students were bused to sixth grade centers and Prime 6 schools, when alternative and vocational schools opened, and when specialized educational programs expanded, more buses and drivers were needed as well. As of CCSD's 50th anniversary, the Transportation Division was equipped with over 1,200 buses, employed almost 1,200 licensed bus drivers, and served 138,000 students daily over 8,000 square miles.

UNLAWFUL TO PASS
when
RED LIGHTS FLASH

Though the terrorist attacks occurred miles from Las Vegas, even the Clark County School District felt their impact. Barbara Edwards, a French and German teacher at Palo Verde High School, was on the American Airlines Flight 77 that crashed into the Pentagon. John Puckett died in the World Trade Center Towers when they were struck by the hijacked airlines. John had been a student in 1964 at Ruby Thomas Elementary School.

Top: John Puckett (r) with B.B. King. Above: Palo Verde ROTC dedicates a memorial for teacher Barbara Edwards.

three college campuses: Henderson (South), Cheyenne (East) and Charleston (West). This unique partnership not only gave students a head start on earning college credits, but it provided additional classroom space and school buildings, again in short supply in the district. As an added bonus, the district covered the cost of the elective college courses, in exchange for not having to provide elective classes for the students at their high schools.

More bonds

With the ups and downs and stress of bringing frequent bond issues before the citizens of Clark County, Dr. Cram came up with a new plan. In 1998, the school district went to the voters with a ten-year bond request, assuring the public the bond would adequately fund the district for the next decade.

Proposing a ten-year bond for $3.5 billion was risky; if it didn't pass, CCSD would be in a difficult spot. Community leaders stepped up and asked for volunteers to get the 1998 bond issue passed. These same leaders sat down with the gaming community and encouraged them to support the bond issue.

This support was important because the 1998 bond sought income from three sources: real estate transfers ($0.60 for every five hundred dollars of the sale price of a real estate transaction), a hotel room tax (1.625 percent), and property taxes. The attractive aspect of the property tax was that it would freeze the rate at $0.5534 per one thousand dollars assessed value for ten years. Voters supported the bond issue by a margin of sixty-five percent.

The $3.5 billion bond issue went toward building eighty-eight new schools and two new bus yards.

Besides new construction, the 1998 bond issue sought to ensure that all schools in Clark County were equipped with similar facilities. Older schools would be rehabilitated to meet up-to-date standards.

Thanks to a booming economy, the bond brought in more revenue than expected, and the Clark County School District was able to build 101 schools, more than the original eighty-eight schools promised.

More money was available beyond the renovation and modernization of 228 schools. Besides adding new classrooms, this money went toward new security systems for the schools, new playground equipment, and access to wide-area networks in each classroom. In addition, telephones were installed in all classrooms and worn furniture was replaced.

It is one thing to build new schools; it is quite another to attract enough teachers to staff the schools. Beginning in 1999, the school district had to

1998 new teacher luncheon.

Superintendent Dr. Brian Cram acts as teacher for a day.

Below left: Carlos Garcia replaces Dr. Cram as Superintendent of CCSD.

Below right: Hispanic supporters at school board meeting endorse Garcia appointment.

hire close to 1,700 new teachers each year. This would be a difficult task in normal times, but there was a major teacher shortage nationwide in the late 1990s; even the local College of Education at the University of Nevada, Las Vegas had experienced a drop in the number of teacher candidates enrolling. Dr. Cram challenged UNLV to increase the number of students enrolling in their teacher training programs. CCSD and UNLV also collaborated on the development of the Paradise Professional School, which put an active CCSD elementary school on the University's campus for in-depth teacher training and experience. By the 1999–2000 school year, the number of teacher candidates doubled.

Yet the CCSD student population continued to grow. Whereas there had been just over 110,000 students enrolled when Dr. Cram first came on board, there were 215,000 students only ten years later, almost double in size. The school district's human resources officials knew they had to think outside the box to entice enough teachers to join the CCSD team. The district employed a variety of marketing tools: posting recruiting posters in airports, setting up video conferences with teaching colleges throughout the country, and setting up a recruitment website. The district even sent video telephones to prospects to be used for interviews. Once enough teachers were hired for a school year, the recruitment race began for the following year. More than one hundred schools had been added in the same ten year period, creating a record for Dr. Cram's superintendency that would probably never be challenged.

Garcia at the helm

After a successful eleven years as superintendent, Cram stepped down in 2000. Carlos Garcia, superintendent of the Fresno Unified School District in California, was selected from a pool of five candidates, delighting the Hispanic community in the valley.

For the first time ever in Clark County, the ethnic minority student population surpassed the former white majority. In 1965, a special study by the Clark County Education Planning Council recorded a student population of eighty-five percent whites and a combination of fifteen percent minorities. At the request of the NAACP another census was taken in 1967, showing a slight decrease in the percentage of white students, to 83.7 percent, and a slight increase in the African American student population, from 10.7 percent to 12.1 percent. Hispanic populations were included with other minorities in that report. By the 2000–2001 school year, the ratio had changed dramatically, with whites representing only 49.6 percent of the student population and Hispanics up from 3.3 percent to twenty-nine percent, a greater increase than African Americans, whose representation grew only to 13.9 percent.

No Child Left Behind

The No Child Left Behind Act (NCLB), passed by Congress in December 2001, had serious repercussions for the CCSD; in the throes of massive population growth, the dramatic change in the language and cultural diversity occurring in Clark County at the time, and struggling with funding issues, this unfunded mandate provided a major challenge to newly-appointed Superintendent Garcia.

The new legislation required all states to test their students annually with the goal of having all students achieving at grade level in reading, language arts, math, and science by 2014, though each state set their own standards and developed their own assessments. Nevada revised its accountability statutes through passage of Senate Bill 1 in the nineteenth special session in June 2003. Students in grades three through eight were now required to be tested annually and at least once during high school.

This analysis of student performance differed from previous measurements in two significant ways: one, test scores were required to be reported for all ethnic subgroups within a school, as well as for subgroups that included low income students, students with disabilities (special education), and students for whom English was their second language; and two, schools would be held accountable for student performance in all subgroups, in all grade levels, and in all areas being tested. Schools failing to reach the targeted goal, called Adequate Yearly Progress (AYP), in just one of these areas were identified as "needing improvement." Schools meeting their goals were labeled "adequate" or "high achieving." No longer was a school's achievement rate based on average scores of the entire student body. Additionally, ability tests (similar to an IQ) were no longer used to determine a child's potential for learning. The No Child Left Behind Act simply stated that all students must achieve at grade level regardless of

The No Child Left Behind Act, passed by Congress in December 2001, had serious repercussions for the CCSD.

The music program is the most notable and successful arts program for CCSD at both elementary and secondary levels. In fact, the variety of music education courses is so comprehensive that almost twenty-three percent of high school students participate in some form of a music program, more than double the national average.

Courses available throughout CCSD:

Advanced Conducting

Advanced Strings

Arranging/ Songwriting

Beginning, Intermediate, Advanced Band

Beginning, Intermediate, Advanced, Ensemble Guitar

Beginning Mariachi & Viheula

Beginning Mariachi & Violin

Chorus

Digital Sound/Music Production

Glee Club

Handbell Ensemble

Jazz Band

Las Vegas Youth Orchestra

Las Vegas Youth Philharmonic

Latin American Music

Latin Pop/Ensemble

Madrigals

Marching Band

Mariachi Ensemble

Modern Music Technology

Music Appreciation

Music History

Music Production

Music Theory

Musical Instrumental Digital Interface Technology (MIDI)

Musical Theatre/ Opera

Orchestra

Percussion Ensemble

Piano

Vocal Ensemble

World Instrumental Music

World Music

The Clark County School District was the first school district in Nevada to implement a formal guitar program. It began with only two classes and exploded to nineteen in just a few years. The classes draw students who otherwise might not be interested in music education.

The Mariachi program is also widely popular. In 2001, the same year the program began, students performed for the Nevada legislature. One of the performers told the legislators how the Mariachi program had saved her life, that before she joined the team, she planned to drop out of school. Mariachi gave her something to look forward to. Instead of dropping out, she attended classes regularly, graduated from high school, and went on to college.

Over two thousand five hundred students are enrolled in the

Mariachi program. This success has not gone unnoticed, capturing the attention of other school districts throughout the nation. The VH1 Save the Music Foundation named the Clark County Board of School Trustees the recipient of the Award for Distinguished Support of Music Education, which is given to only one school board in the nation a year. In addition, the National Association of Music Merchants named the Clark County School District as the most supportive district of music education. CCSD was also named as one of the top one hundred school districts for music education six years running.

The humanities/drama program is a newer edition to CCSD's elementary arts education curriculum. In 2002, ten humanities/drama teachers were placed at larger schools. By the fiftieth anniversary of the Clark County School District, eighty drama teachers were in the elementary schools in the district. The success of these programs is reflected in the growth of award-winning theatrical productions and performances at the high school level.

In 1987, CCSD created a curriculum that employed a holistic approach to aesthetics, art criticism, art history, and art production. The district's commitment to early visual arts education contributed to its tremendous popularity with secondary students. Its success is evident throughout the community; student work can be found in public buildings and McCarran International Airport.

Silvestri Junior High School Jazz Band.

The Global Community High School opened in August 2005 to provide educational services to high school students who have been in the United States less than two years and speak little or no English. In addition to English immersion and academic classes, students take an acculturation class, which acquaints them with basic living skills: banking, public transportation, simple English phrases, among other details of day-to-day living in the US.

of Reading First grants to lower socio-economic schools that were not eligible for Title I funds.

Supporters of the NCLB Act pointed to improved test scores in reading and math for nine-year-olds by the end of 2005. In fact, according to NAEP results (National Assessment of Educational Progress), there was greater improvement from 2000 to 2005 than in the previous twenty-eight years combined. The achievement gap between whites and African Americans and whites and Hispanics was also at an all-time low.

Critics of NCLB argued that the focus on standardized, multiple-choice testing encouraged teachers to teach a shallow subset of skills rather than focus on deeper understanding of concepts. There was also concern that the majority of instruction time was spent testing students, and while many educators acknowledged that the amount of time spent teaching reading, writing, and math had increased, time for teaching the arts, physical education, social studies, and humanities had decreased, thereby providing children with a less well-rounded education.

There had always been a collaboration between elementary and secondary education, but in 2001, Superintendent Garcia structured the curriculum more uniformly through the levels. By aligning kindergarten through the twelfth grade standards, the school district was able to articulate comprehensive

race, language difference, socio-economic level, ability or disability.

School districts were required to comply with this federal mandate or jeopardize their federal funding for education. The Clark County School District began putting systems in place that would give teachers feedback regarding their students' progress on curriculum benchmarks frequently during the year. Interim tests were also developed in addition to the typical year-end curriculum tests (CRT, Writing Assessment, or the High School Proficiency Examinations). The Instructional Data Management System (IDMS), new technology software, allowed teachers to analyze group progress and track test data for each student's entire school career. Some added federal funding for NCLB came in the form

educational goals and encourage communication between teachers of different grade levels.

In March 2002, Superintendent Garcia addressed the dropout rate of Hispanic students. At the time, Hispanics made up just over thirty percent of the high school student body, but their dropout rate was fifty percent higher than the school district's average. CCSD had a shortage of TESL-endorsed (teachers of English as a second language) teachers to address the needs of the sixty-seven thousand students who were not fluent English speakers. Garcia noted that this number could grow to ninety thousand children. He promised that the Clark County School District would address the concerns of non-English speaking students in the coming year.

In an effort to diffuse interest in splitting CCSD into several districts, Garcia reorganized CCSD into five regions that supervised and coordinated elementary, middle, and high schools within those regions in an effort to create better transition for students from one level of school experience to the next. Administrative centers were built in each of the five regions of the district to better address the needs of schools and foster parental input.

Augustin Orci, co-interim superintendent, 2005.

Dr. Walt Rulffes, co-interim superintendent, 2005 and superintendent, 2005—present.

Garcia also proposed block scheduling in high schools with high percentages of credit deficient students in an attempt to provide additional credit retrieval opportunities, and mandated an "Algebra by 8" philosophy in the hope that more students would pass the Nevada proficiency exam in mathematics required for a high school diploma.

While Garcia's ideas for educational improvement were impressive, concern grew over their practicality and ability to deliver the promised outcomes, and soon budget constraints hampered his efforts. Many programs were cut, creating larger class sizes and eliminating middle school athletics. In 2005, Garcia, who had originally said he planned to spend ten years in Las Vegas and retire from CCSD, left the state to work for McGraw-Hill Publishers.

Career and technical education

The state legislature passed the Nevada Education Reform Act of 1997, which provided funding to put a computer in all nine thousand of Nevada's classrooms. Today, computers are a vital part of the educational experience in the Clark County School District. New school standard equipment lists now include a variety of versatile computers, powerful file servers, printers, scanners, digital cameras, smart boards, and other cutting edge technologies for use in computer labs, classrooms, offices, and libraries.

CCSD delivers classes over the Internet to help students living in rural areas and those with full work schedules get their high school diploma online. The first class of the virtual high school graduated in 2005.

Right: Chef Wolfgang Puck works with culinary students at the Career and Technical Academy.

Year after year, state statistics demonstrate that students in career and technical education (CTE) programs have a significantly lower dropout rate than their counterparts in general education. Using funds appropriated by the 2005 (and 2007) legislative session to support the enhancement of CTE programs, the Clark County School District initiative has set the lead in the state, and indeed in the nation, for designing and building new career and technical academies. These state-of-the-art facilities will allow students access to quality CTE programs that reflect industry needs and meet new technology standards. Guided by the principle that all students need to be prepared for careers as well as college, the curriculum at these schools are being created in collaboration with postsecondary faculty and representatives of the business and industry community. CTE students in CCSD also may earn college credits for designated courses articulated with the College of Southern Nevada.

Superintendents during this era: Brian Cram, 1989-2000; Carlos Garcia, 2000-2005; Walt Rulffes, 2005-present

Dr. Rulffes

In the summer of 2005, Augustin Orci, Deputy Superintendent of Instruction for CCSD, and Dr. Walt Rulffes, CCSD's Deputy Superintendent of Business, stepped in to serve as the district's co-interim superintendents. Dr. Rulffes also remained responsible for the fiscal management of the district's multi-billion dollar budget and the 1998 capital improvement program, which was the largest programs of its kind in the nation.

The Clark County School District Board of Trustees voted unanimously to offer Dr. Rulffes the position as CCSD's tenth superintendent, which became effective January 26, 2006. Dr. Rulffes had been in CCSD since 1998, when he was hired by Superintendent Brian Cram to become Chief Financial Officer. Dr. Rulffes' previous experience as superintendent of the Cheney School District in Washington, as well as the knowledge he had acquired about Nevada's and Clark County's education funding model and the district's capital improvement plan, gave him a solid background in both education and finance the board was seeking in a new superintendent.

One of Dr. Rulffes' first decisions created the Superintendent's schools, a division to oversee magnet schools, career and technical centers, and empowerment schools, which were designed to improve student performance through increased autonomy and accountability, smaller class sizes, a longer school day and year, and more financial support. Schools designated "empowerment" have greater control over their individual school budgets; in addition to state education funds, they receive six-hundred dollars per student from the district, and fifty-thousand dollars from a community partner for the school to invest. The Lincy Foundation recently gave CCSD a grant for three years to support the concept of empowerment schools. The expectation is that student achievement will increase dramatically with more local control of the budget and dedicated community involvement.

Schools built 1995–2005

Elementary Schools:
O.K. Adcock (new building)
Tony Alamo
Dean La Mar Allen
John C. Bass
Kathy L. Batterman
James Bilbray
John W. Bonner
Joseph L. Bowler
Eileen Brookman
Richard H. Bryan
Roger M. Bryan
Berkley L. Bunker
Arturo Cambeiro
Kay Carl
Roberta Curry Cartwright
Eileen Conners
Manuel Cortez
Steve Cozine
Marshall Darnell
Ollie Detwiler
Raul Elizondo
Charles Frias
Edith Garehime
Roger Gehring
Linda R. Givens
Daniel Goldfarb
Judy & John Goolsby
Theron & Naomi Goynes
Addelair D. Guy
Keith & Karen Hayes
Howard Heckethorn

Liliam Lujan Hickey
Howard Hollingsworth
John R. Hummel
Mervin Iverson
Jay W. Jeffers
Lorna Kesterson
Frank Lamping
Reynaldo Martinez
Sandy Miller
William K. Moore
Sue H. Morrow
Joseph M. Neal
D'Vorre & Hall Ober
Paradise (new building)
Dean Peterson
Richard Priest
Betsy A. Rhodes
Aldeane Comito Ries
Aggie Roberts
Lucile Rogers
William & Ma Scherkenbach
Eva Simmons
Hal Smith
William Snyder
Ethel Staton
Sunrise Acres (new building)
Wayne Tanaka
Sheila Tarr
John Tartan
Glen Taylor
Joseph E. Thiriot
Neil Twitchell

John C. Vanderburg
Virgin Valley (new building)
J. Marlan Walker
Fredric Watson
Elizabeth Wilhelm
Eva Wolfe
Elise Wolff

Middle Schools:
Dr. William H. Bailey
Ralph Cadwallader
H. & L. Canarelli
Francis H. Cortney
Brian & Teri Cram
Victoria Fertitta
Clifford Findlay
Kathleen &Tim Harney
Charles Hughes
Duane D. Keller
Clifford Lawrence
Justice Myron E. Leavitt
Lied
Jerome D. Mack
Jack & Terry Mannion
Bob Miller
Irwin & Susan Molasky
Mario & Joanne Monaco
Sig Rogich
Anthony Saville
Jack Schofield
Marvin Sedway
Charles Silvestri

Del E. Webb
Charles I. West

High Schools:
Arbor View
Canyon Springs
Centennial
Coronado
Del Sol
Desert Pines
Foothill
Liberty
Mojave
Palo Verde
Shadow Ridge
Sierra Vista
Spring Valley

Alternative/Special Schools:
Cowan Behavioral Junior/Senior High

CCSD Enrollment 1956–2005

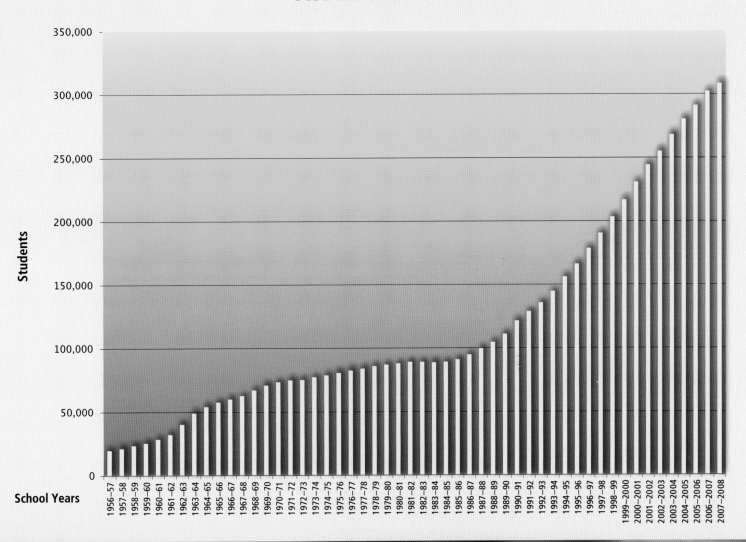

Afterword

It is doubtful anyone could have predicted that a tiny railroad stop in the middle of the desert would become a world-renowned resort destination, let alone be home to over three hundred thousand students.

Yet fifty years later, the Clark County School District continues to grow and flourish, facing the challenges of providing for new students while maintaining standards for the existing student population. With optimism and dedication, CCSD's commitment to excellence in education will survive another fifty years.

Acknowledgments

Without the wealth of information provided by the following individuals, this book would not be complete. Their detailed analyses, valuable contacts, and personal anecdotes enriched the research previously gathered. The Clark County School District's 50th Anniversary Archive Committee would like to thank:

Susan Alesevich	Charlene Green		
Rollie Armstrong	Joan Greenberg		
Tom Axtell	Dianne Greene		
Maureen Benjamin	Linda Gregg		
Pat Bickhart	Joyce Haldeman		
Judy Cameron	DeLloyd Hammond		
Mike Campbell	Gary Handelman		
Helen Cannon	Hazel Handelman	Barbara Misday	Diane Reitz
Allin Chandler	Kathy Harney	Ray Mitchell	Ron Ross
Marjorie Conner	Deb Hegna	Helene Monahan	Thomas Sarno
Dorothy Courtemanche	Rosemary Holmes-Gull	John Morgan	Bobby Seals
Norm Craft	Jacqueline Jaeger	Shirl Neagle	Mike Shaw
Kay Cromeenes	Jane Kadoich	Marcia Neel	Tom Shimer
Donna Cuda	Ron Keller	Michelle Nelson	Lois Tarkanian
Sharon Datoli	Geri Kodey	Leland Newcomer	Ransom Terrell
Dusty Dickens	Jim Larsen	Nadine Nielsen	Charles Thompson
Ryan Dwyer	Larry Lochridge	Agustin Orci	Martha Tittle
Jhone Ebert	Thalia Dondero	Dennis Ortwein	Virginia "Beezy" Lani Tobiasson
Leanne Ferdig	Marilyn Dondero Loop	Joyce Ostrowski	Pat Van Betten
Kathleen Frosini	Nila Marchant	Jane Bunker Overy	Marty Vodovoz
Betty Gallifent	William Marchant	Carl Partridge	Alice Wisdom
Galen Good	Dennis McBride	Kip Patterson	Dode Worsham
Gary Gray	Peter Michel	Claude Perkins	Virginia Young

CCSD 50th Anniversary Fund

In addition, the Archive Committee would like to express their appreciation to the following individuals and businesses that contributed to the CCSD's 50th Anniversary Fund, chaired by Frank Lamping and Charles Silvestri. Their financial support made this project possible.

Platinum Contributors
Cox Communications
Station Casinos

Gold Contributors
Anderson Dairy, Inc.
International Brotherhood of
  Electrical Workers Local
Nevada Power Company
Republic Services of Southern
  Nevada

Silver Contributors
John & Betty Gallifent
Sierra Health Services
Yamaha Corporation of America

Bronze Contributors
Alliant Healthcare Services
Bishop Gorman High School Fund
  Development
Bradsaw Smith & Company, LLP
CPR Connection
Domingo Cambeiro Corporation
Don Hayden
Howard Core Company, LLC
Harold Bernheisel

Howard Core Company, LLC
JMA Architecture Studios
Kamico Instructional Media, Inc.
Klassy Kids, Inc.
Lawrenceville Press, Inc.
LVGRADS Lance K. Shoen
Modtech Holdings
North American Video, Inc.
Teacher to Teacher.com
TJK Consulting Engineers, Inc.
Welles Pugsley Architects, LLP

Friends
American Fidelity Assurance
  Company
Aspinall Inc. dba Frame of Mind
Harold Bernheisel
Kay Carl
Patrick Carlton
Chartu
Class.com, Inc.
Committee to Elect Joe Hardy
DGI David Gragg Dales, Inc.
Thalia M. Dondero
Educational Achievement Services,
  Inc.
Elbern Publications

Executive Strategies, LLC
Flagtime, USA
Flowers by Michelle, Inc.
Kay S. Fulton
John E. Genasci
The Graphic Edge
M.L. Greenfield
Keith Harper
Instruction Logic, Inc.
International Commercial Supply
    Corporation, LLC
Invo Healthcare Associates, Inc.
J & J Marketing, Inc.
L.A. Steelcraft Products, Inc.
Learning Solutions
M2 Services, LLC dba Hunter
    Service Company
Mach One Enterprises, LLC
Steven D. McCoy
Meadow Gold Dairies
Ridgefields Brand Corporation
Sahara Camera Center
Carmen Salcedo
Sam Ash Music Corporation and
    Affiliates
Sandberg & Small dba SSA
    Architecture
Gene Segerblom
Spectra Rep, Inc.

Sports Imports
Jean Stewart
Trade Show Services, Ltd. Dba
    Pro-Tect Security
Tropicana Hotel & Casino
Unity School Bus Parts, Inc.
Walker Specialty Construction, Inc.
Wawona Frozen Foods
Valerie Weiner

**CCSD 50th Anniversary
Committee Members**
Helene Amos
Susan Brager-Wellman
Ralph Cadwallader
Kay Carl
Patrick Carlton
Thalia Dondero
Kathy Foster
John Gallifent
Edward Greer
Sandie M. Harmony
Don Hayden
Charlotte Hill
Terri D. Janison
Craig Kadlub
Michael L. Kinnaird
Ken Kopolow
Frank Lamping

Jaime Lea
Karlene Lee
Holli K. Kalaleh
Bruce Miller
Pat Nelson
Joe Phillips
Nancy E. Schkurman
Candy Schneider
Charles Silvestri
Eva G. Simmons
Judi Steele
Gail Taksel
Wayne Tanaka
Rick Watson
Thurman White
James T. Williams
Joyce L. Woodhouse
Dan Wray

CCSD Archive Committee
Helene Amos
Charlene Bolyard
Kay Carl
John Gallifent
Don Hayden
Pat Nelson
Julie Newberry
Donna Perkins
Joe Phillips
Dayle Rust
Cynthia Sell
Rick Watson
Jim Williams
Dan Wray

About the Archive Committee

The Archive Committee is comprised of retired Clark County School District educators who are dedicated to collecting, cataloging, and preserving information and materials that are pertinent to the history of the CCSD. The Archive Committee has worked diligently to create a permanent collection of fifty years of documents, maps, photography, and other memorabilia, as well as establish a foundation for future generations of educators to continue to archive artifacts and record our history. In addition, the 50th Anniversary Committee purchased display cases that are located in the lobby of the CCSD Administration building on West Sahara, where the Archive Committee will be able to showcase new information and items that contributed to the history of the district.

Harvey Dondero

John Gallifent
CCSD Photographer 1964–1973

Rollie Armstrong
CCSD Photographer 1974–1991

Geri Kodey
CCSD Photographer 1991–2002

Pat Nelson

Special Acknowledgments

Quite simply, this book would not have been possible without the dedication of the following individuals:

John Gallifent, Rollie Armstrong, and Geri Kodey, the Clark County School District photographers whose visual documentation of the district's history has brought *Education in the Neon Shadow* to life;

Associate Superintendent Harvey Dondero, who, in addition to his other duties, supervised the CCSD Photo Department for over twenty years. His support and encouragment inspired the collection of more than 30,000 photographs and color slides of

district activities and events; and Pat Nelson, who inherited supervision of the photo department after several district reorganizations. When the department was dissolved about 2002 and materials were going to the dump, Pat rescued all the negatives and slides and had her staff begin to index them all. Then in 2005 as planning began for the fiftieth anniversary, Pat had the idea of creating a commemorative book. The first meetings with Stephen Press were with Pat and the archive committee.

We hope current and future CCSD staff will be inspired to preserve their history as well.

References

Bancroft, Herbert Howe. *History of Nevada 1540–1888.* University of Nevada Press, Reno, Nevada, 1981.

Bowler, G. Lynn. *Zion On The Muddy.* Art City Publishing, Springdale, Utah, 2004.

Conant, James B. *The American High School Today.* McGraw-Hill Book Company, 1959.

Davis, Sam P., Editor. *History of Nevada.* Vol. 1 and 2, 1912. Reprinted by Nevada Publications, Las Vegas, Nevada, 1984.

Dondero, Harvey N. *History of Clark County Schools.* 1986.

Dunar/McBride. *Building Hoover Dam.* University of Nevada Press, 1993.

Edwards, Elbert B. *200 Years in Nevada.* Publishers Press, Salt Lake City, Utah, 1978.

Flesch, Rudolf. *Why Johnny Can't Read And What You Can Do About It.* Harper, 1955.

Haenszel, Arda M. *Searchlight Remembered.* Tales of the Mojave Road Publishing Company, Norco, California 1988.

Kline, Morris. *Why Johnny Can't Add: The Failure of the New Math.* Random House, Inc., 1974.

Mooney, Courtney. *Las Vegas Centennial Celebration* brochure. City of Las Vegas Planning and Development Department, 2005.

Ravitch, Diane. Left Back: *A Century of Failed School Reforms.* Simon & Schuster, 2000.

Warren, Liz and Courtney Mooney. *Pioneer Trail* brochure. City of Las Vegas Arts Commission, City of Las Vegas Planning & Development Department, Comprehensive Planning Division, Historic Preservation Commission.

Photo Credits:

Blue Diamond History Committee
Boulder City Museum
City of Henderson Archives and Records
Clark County School District Photographic Archives
Leanne Ferdig Family Collection
Goodsprings Historical Society
Las Vegas Review-Journal
Library of Congress
National Archives
Old Logandale School Historical and Cultural Society
Searchlight Museum & Guild Archives
University of Nevada, Las Vegas Special Collections
Vegas PBS

Clark County School District 50th Anniversary
Namesake Celebration
October 11, 2006

Namesake honorees; the names behind the faces:

Front Row (left to right)
Cannon, Helen
Faiss, Theresa
Faiss, Wilbur
Jeffers, Jay
Monaco, JoAnn
Heckethorn, Howard
Katz, Edyth
Von Tobel, Ed
Molasky, Irwin
Hickey Liliam
Thiriot, Joseph
Ober, D'Vorre
Ober, Hal
Givens, Linda Rankin
Hollingsworth, Howard
Goynes, Naomi
Parson, Stella

Second Row (left to right)
Escobedo Sr., Edmundo
Wolff, Elise L.
Steele, Judy
Hayes, Karen
Harney, Kathleen
Molasky, Susan
Lynch, Ann
Hill, Charlotte
Carl, Kay
Swainston, Theron
Twitchell, Neil
Watson, Rick
Iverson, Mervin
Fertitta, Victoria
Alamo, Tony
Goynes, Theron
Priest, Richard

Third Row (left to right)
Simmons, Eva
Harney, Tim
Greer, Edward A.
White, Thurman
Lamping, Frank
Jeffrey, Jack

Back Row (left to right)
Monaco, Mario
Lawrence, Clifford
Darnell, Marshall
Wallace, Matt
Tanaka, Wayne
Schorr, Steve
Mendoza, John F.
Mannion, Terry
Mannion, Jack
Gehring, Roger
Saville, Anthony
Bilbray, James
Dickens, Dusty
Roundy, Owen
Cortney, Francis
Ries, Aldeane
Johnston, Carroll
Bailey, Dr. William "Bob"